Just when I was worried that New York City might be done—stick a fork in that homogenized purlieu of financiers and trust-fund hipsters!—the Big Apple offers up a bohemian original to remind us that groundbreaking artists can still thrive in sidewalk cracks, like Marianne Moore's strawberry that's had a struggle. John Marcus Powell's *Glorious Babe* is the book W. H. Auden might have written (in the vein of "The Platonic Blow") after inviting Catullus up for a night of love. What shocks and unsettles most in Powell's audacious—and audaciously musical—poems is not their nostalgia for the glory days of Glory Holes and the "Teeny-Pervs" and "Hooli-girlie-gans" of Christopher Street but how much our needs and obsessions are mirrored by this array of con artists, fine artists, fine friends, and glorious babes. Powell's forthrightly Queer and queerly forthright collection (with glorious illustrations by Julio M. Perea) affirms, more than any other recent book I can think of, that the job of the poet is, like Trelawney on the beach at Viareggio, to reach into the pyre and seize hold of the human heart.

David Yezzi (author, Birds Of The Air)

Many of us may begin life as glorious babes, but few will end up as glorious and uproarious in our declining years as John Marcus Powell. In these poems he lifts the lid on life and love, demonstrating effortlessly that they are one and the same thing. He gives me special pleasure with his wicked insights into the pretensions of a place where he lived once and I live now. I have laughed delightedly till my lungs ache, but this self-inflicted discomfort is not severe enough to account for the occasional tears, which took me by surprise.

Ann Drysdale (author, Quaintness And Other Offences)

There is not a boring word in the book.
The book does not satiate. A sequel would be welcome.

Tom Merrill (author, Facing The Remains)

GLORIOUS BABE

GLORIOUS BABE

Poems by

JOHN MARCUS POWELL

EXOT BOOKS
2014

EXOT BOOKS
NEW YORK

2 Rugby Road
Massapequa, NY 11758
www.exottreasures.com/exotbooks

First Edition
Copyright 2014 Exot Books
All Rights Reserved
Typeset in Book Antiqua & Britannic Bold
ISBN: 978-0-9898984-1-6

Illustration and Book Design: Julio M. Perea
Cover Photos: Julio M. Perea
Editor: R. Nemo Hill

ACKNOWLEDGMENTS
Exot Books is grateful to the these print and online journals where versions of the following poems first appeared:

Shit Creek Review —
St. Vincent

Big City Lit —
If A Boyfriend Comes In With New Pants

The Hypertexts —
Who Is Your Favorite Royal?, Showroom,
My Abode, Tenant Patrol, Thin Skinned,
Nature Of Questions, I Met Julia Childs,
The Bottom Of Christopher Street,
More Visitors To The Pacific Northwest

Faroutfurtheroutofsight —
Tenant Patrol

The main shapes Arise!
Shapes of democracy total, result of centuries,
Shapes ever projecting other shapes,
Shapes of Turbulent manly cities,

— Walt Whitman

~

These poems are dedicated to:

Walter Cox
R. Nemo Hill
Jennifer Humphrey

When I lose direction
and forget what I need to write,
these friends are 'The Shapes That Arise'
to show me the way.

Table Of Contents

PREFACE / xv

1
GLORIOUS BABE

Glorious Babe / 1
Soldier / 3
Anonymity / 6
Politics / 8
Teaching English As A Foreign Language / 10
Who Is Your Favorite Royal? / 13
I Met Julia Childs / 16
Hiding / 19
Pretending / 21
I Wish I Belonged To This Story / 24

2
PRIVATE VIEW

Private View / 29
Muscled Mounties / 31
Master Of The Hurricane / 33
Trip To Paradise / 35
Tenant Patrol / 38
Tenant Patrol Redux / 40
Summers In New York / 42
Prevailing Sensations / 43
Jane's Husband / 45
Disposables / 48
Casual Public Exhibitionist / 50
Emails / 53
Searching For Str8 Bi Married Tops On The DL / 55
Showroom / 57
Smile / 59
My Abode / 61

3
NATURE OF QUESTIONS

    Nature Of Questions / 65
    If A Boyfriend Comes In With New Pants / 68
    Incident On The Roof, 2001 / 70
    Mille-Feuille / 72
    Extra Work / 74
    Water Boarding / 77
    Amish Country / 79
    August Visitor To The Pacific Northwest / 82
    More Visitors To The Pacific Northwest / 84

4
CHANGING

    Changing / 89
    Helen's Gone / 91
    Helen Has Returned / 93
    End Of The Affair / 96
    Thin Skinned / 98
    Work Ethic / 100
    Polish and Moroccan Constructions / 103
    Rehab In Westchester / 105
    Saint Vincent / 108
    Taste / 110
    Pagan Rights / 111
    The Bottom Of Christopher Street / 113

Preface

The narrative is rife with languid detour, the subject often scandalous, and the language inflected with the sort of eccentrically personal rigor that can never be counterfeited.

The style is one-of-a-kind, they-broke-the-mould, genre-less, self-tailored, one-size-fits-no-one-but—, one-line-barely-fits-in-the-margins-of-the-goddamned-page. Perhaps those who have heard the tone and timber of the live voice will be less surprised by the switchbacks and U-turns, by the comet trails and off-the-map collisions of these lines of print—but even they will never entirely escape from delicious bewilderments when confronted with the irrefutable evidence of these unruly texts jostling for paper parking space. The tempo is *allegro attenuato*.

Crimes are committed affably, forgiven fervently, exploited shamelessly. And those who commit them are liberally rewarded—though, most often, with nothing more tangible than the family jewels.

The jewels are somewhat tarnished, but still scintillating in proper light. That the proper lighting is not always available is a fact faced without petulance or regret. The cookies crumble, the milk spills, the planes crash and burn, the lies drift and settle, but Helen more-often-than-not returns with at least a horse-and-half-full of hot men.

The cry is one part *cock-a-doodle-doo*, to two parts *koo-koo-ka-choo*. The flavor is somewhere between absinthe and strong black tea. The music is Mahler's lost symphony for solo accordion. Occasionally there are *jalapeños* in the dark, merciful mineral waters in the white wine, bothersome gravels in the kidney, and a mushroom cloud on the horizon. The voice is more audible the more intimately it whispers. There is, at times, a bit of spittle—yet the saliva itself is a rare blend, a deep rich brew of sea foam on distant shores, of Bardic dews and daring oral vaudevilles.

Sacred cows and lambs *are* led to slaughter, stuffed, spiced, braised, sometimes even pickled—then served with loaves & fishes & chips & anti-retro-virals in the lobbies and restrooms of hospitals and community centers of ill repute. One is convinced that no *real* animals were harmed in the making of these poems.

The man in these poems, the poet in residence, is irresponsibly irrepressible, his wit barbed with warmth, his bait compulsively edible, his verve seemingly infinite. The Coat of Arms is Torch *Argent*, on Field *Azul*, within Cracked Heart *Oro*: silver torch, blue field, heart of gold. The motto, in Letters *Négro* on Banner *Lavender*, translated from the original Latin reads as follows: "*Stitched with honor, oft besmirched—*" followed, in pencil, by a phone number and an obscene suggestion scribbled in an almost illegible script. Scholars contend that this was added at a later date, perhaps as recently as yesterday.

Like any well or reservoir, the water at the top can be brackishly intoxicating, sweet and sour with season upon season of ferment. Yeasty and lusty on the surface, various objects can be found floating in the pool from time to time—empty beers cans and tequila bottles, dead leaves and insects, an old jockstrap, the cellophane wrappers of candy accepted from strangers, the usual scums and jisms of a life led to the fullest. But for those not averse to the occasional dive into murky waters, the realms below are cool and clear with the welcome sting of sobriety after an equally welcome debauch. To all potential readers, and they should be legion, I say: "*Drink up, boys and girls! This is how it is done!*"

R. Nemo Hill
May—2014

1
GLORIOUS BABE

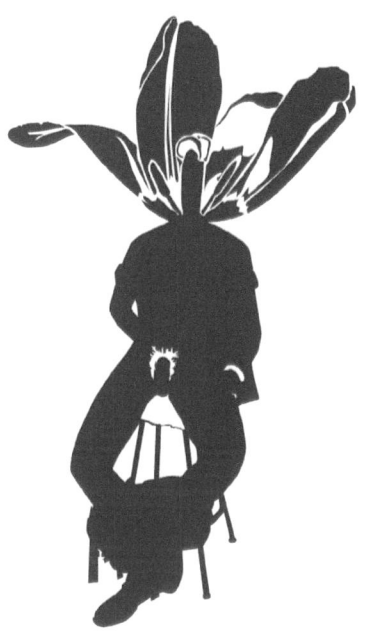

*Here they will whistle for the storm,
and the Sodom and the Solymas,
and the wild beasts and the armies.*

– Rimbaud
(trans, Louise Varese)

Glorious Babe

As a thank-you
for his Mam's decision not to abort him
Herman was born a Glorious Babe,
and took pains to grow into a complicated man.
At a year old, his Mam took him
to the great photographer in the high street,
the sole photographer in town —
to sit for his photo.

Straight up sitting.
Legs stretched out in front along.
Wearing zilch. With freak moon nipples,
and the dumpling planets of his bum and tum.
There is no weakness.
The Babe is purity.
The Babe is ardent hunky baby brawn.

The photographer displays the photo in his window.
Under deft lighting it's a primitive image,
more natural than Nature, superior to Man.

Aldermen and alderwomen,
farm laborers with milk maidens,
workers from the munitions factory,
paroled prisoners, the insane,
all reckon the Babe to be an Oracle —
indicating innocence in the vicinity,
glory in the town.

For decades the Babe has a place of honor
in the spacious window,
his smile rejecting the lavish claustrophobia of cities
and of womb.
On market days, citizens conglomerate in the high street
to glimpse the photo,
but don't connect the image with Herman as he walks along.
Herman (grown older) wonders,
"Is life a diversion? And what's to come?"

There was a shattering
in the evening of the century —
an arm was thrust through the red velvet
that hides the studio at the rear of the window.
In the peculiar interval twixt non-realization and realization,
the photo, flat under glass, was gone!
Faith disintegrates in the small metropolis.
Reasons are given — Disbelief in religion! Decomposition! War!

The memory of the Babe's body and the Babe's face
conjures on the mountain,
in the shop fronts,
in the town hall —
it enters the fishmonger's
and adheres to a counter of blanched marble
where a slather of seaweed, sodden ebony,
temporarily belongs.

A culinary feature of the area,
this seaweed, mashed to a pulp,
is shaped into cakes, then fried.
The seaweed is on the menu in Herman's restaurant.
When its taste explodes in the mouth, it has much in common
with a turbulent mystery, with a criminal sigh.

Soldier

Abergavenny is my home town.
In Welsh, *Aber* translates as *mouth*.
Gavenny is the name of a river.

Therefore, Abergavenny signifies *Mouth of The Gavenny River*. Then again the Gavenny isn't a river. It's a driblet—starting in the Black Mountains—dribbling—through the cricket field—past the asylum. At the bus station, before traversing the River Fields to meld into The River Usk, it becomes a brook. This River Usk is large enough to be a real river. Cattle, horses, sheep—drink and nibble. Other creatures indistinguishable. Blackbirds are blackberries when viewed from a far position.

When as a teenager I bathed in the river
water squelched like mercury,
the sun a white knot.

Wikipedia informs
that Abergavenny's history
has had intermittent scandals.

In 1230 there was a massacre in the Norman castle. But nowhere is there any mention of the scandal in the 1940's, when members of the town council (all male) were discovered to enjoy dressing up as women at council meetings in the town hall.

A percentage of the council
transformed into the feminine principle.
The rest stayed as they were.

These goings on were photographed
by the owner of the café opposite,
from his balcony.

He telephoned the national press. All over Britain (this was before Britain had become The United Kingdom) images were circulated of the balding Abergavenny Council—bejeweled, bewigged, flaunting floral dresses with stitched-on lace.

> Reflecting the confusion
> of town dressmakers,
> confusion did abound.

> My grandmother was adamant.
> "Never reveal
> you come from Abergavenny!"

"They'll believe you're a Goddamn Nancy who enjoys a *you-know-what* up your goddamn *what's-it*.....I can't bear to think about it....." (She loved thinking about it. When she was drunk she'd hit her own head at her own enjoyments—vivid enough to be happening now.)

> It's my eighteenth summer.
> I have a job at the clothiers
> on the high street.

On a day off, I go to Barry Island—a sea side town. I've already worked out the implications of my Grandmother's warning and so, entering a fish & chips shop with money in my pocket, I am fully prepared when a soldier carrying his cod and chips order and having a choice of 40 vacant chairs around 10 isolated tables in the available shop asks, "Mind if I sit down?" Before sitting, he clips off his belt (like the rest of his uniform, satisfyingly military) and the clunk of the buckle on the tiles of the table bounces onto the fish & chip cooker's cool steel, and is reflected in imitation glass panels resembling mirrors around the top halves of all four walls.

> "Where do you come from?"
> I whisper:
> *"Abergavenny."*

And the table's edge is the edge of my precipice.
And the vinegar will moisten momentous events.
And the salt is a plunge into political meanderings.

> Giving birth
> to the taste of
> "Ask, and I'll tell."

Anonymity

"Anonymity is best expressed in anonymous sex. Beware of kinsfolk!
Depend on the kindness of strangers who say they are friends."

An acquaintance adopted by a rich family
is informed by said family that his birth Mother is Jewish —
a poor unmarried girl from the East End.

His Christian adoptive family is wealth incorporated;
their house, history ingranulated;
his elite Catholic school
embroidered into the fibers of a future career,
into various presidencies and beyond.
In church, pastors give sermons on the nature of suffering
concluding that the human animal gets what it deserves!
Thus my acquaintance learns, and concludes
one should be thankful for laughter.
For laughter, and the touch of another, put him in contact
with what's called *ardor*.
Ardor is the strange innocence of clowns.

Not to worry.
Nearby, below street level, is a public lavatory.
At the bottom of the steps a scent of excretions
doesn't preclude hoary stimulations
at the side-by-side urinals where disaffected bodies
are touched back to life
as in the switching on of a light —
though less the entire body beautiful, than the beautifully
affected parts.

He obtains his mother's maiden name
from the adoption papers.
Instructed by his Christian family that this Jewish mother
must NOT be contacted till his Christian family is in the grave,
he sets about searching immediately
(birth certificates, synagogue where she married, etc, etc)
and discovers his Jewish Mum lives in an adjacent area
two miles up the road.

His birth Mother's house
is as big as the house of his adoptive parents.
Furthermore, she wears wigs with the set of a helmet.
If she was penniless when she popped him,
poverty is now an hypothesis.
In a big car she has a prominent husband
who comes and goes.
My acquaintance follows husband and wife to a synagogue
where suffering is synonymous with quality
and conservation is the tone!

Not to worry.
The synagogue is opposite *The Heath*,
also known as *The Common*.
Leaving the synagogue on a winter's night,
he wanders onto this *Common,*
well aware that this tract, apparently waste,
belongs to mankind in general —
it is *common* ground.

There he meets a Commoner who possesses a guttural grunt,
in that zone of pleasure
where touch equals taste equals sound.
All sense is embedded in the Commoner and him,
him and the Commoner searching, navigating.

What is left of *ardor* beneath the sins of their Christian skins
(which deny the pump of their blood)
has a Talmudic thump-ga-thump-ga-thump
that bounds of its own accord through the immeasurable
within.

Politics

My town on the Welsh border is working class —
yet when election time comes round, the citizens honor
autocratic tastes.
However bent the back of the farm worker,
blistered the hand of the laborer,
undernourished the children and children's teacher —
a Conservative is invariably re-elected to Parliament.

One summer evening I was being driven around
by a policeman, conservative to his corpuscles,
to his square nails, to his cut of hair.
He was married with children, but our friendship
(when I was in school and two years after)
was founded on rip-roaring sexual play.

His suggestion was to drive to an isolated area.
We drove to the top
and then down the sloping back of a mountain,
till this isolated area appeared —
a clump of groping, passionate trees.

On the backside of said mountain
we passed through Tredegar,
a famed Labor constituency.
In those days Labor meant Socialist —
in those days the Marxist shine (we're talking Utopian)
hadn't yet shined its sheen away.

The member of Parliament for Tredegar was Aneurin Bevan,
an ex-miner Socialist icon
who instigated the National Health Service.
"The measure of a civilized society is how it cares for those in need."

On the other hand, there would always be a Game proceeding —
one which Aneurin Bevan wanted to *win*
if only because he *played*.
Aneurin always made a stop in our town
on his way home from Parliament.
There, behind our cattle market,

he got out of his chauffeur-driven Bentley
and into a small Austin driven by a woman
supposed to be his secretary —
thus entering his constituency on the mountain
with ostensible humility.

My policeman took this to be Socialist hypocrisy —
implying he himself personified the contrary.
I was just a kid,
and this policeman was the nearest I came to having a lover.
So I smiled...

...at Aneurin Bevan's politics
and its profane manipulations,
at my policeman's politics
which were just as soiled,
and at my own political stance
founded on the wondrous formations
beneath his police uniform or his tighter-than-tight jeans.

I wasn't a politician, but
I had the propensity to agree, to please.

Teaching English
As A Foreign Language

In the mid '60s I was a sought after actor
but by the end of the decade couldn't get arrested.
This had to do with being Queer and playing straight parts.
Queerness reared in my Straightness.
In my Straightness, Queerness glowed.

Changing direction, I took a course
—TEACHING ENGLISH AS A FOREIGN LANGUAGE—
at a London Institute famous for speculations such as,
"Can language react at a height of its own?"

The Professor was a writer
of English language teaching books.
He'd always say: "My books are only a beginning. Teach
from your own experience." Yet his course books
(entitled *Practical Performances*)
didn't have a single homosexual in them—
though he was as Gay as high-heeled shoes!
His books dealt with a family, the *Family Jones*.
With sketched figures we're told:
"Mrs. Jones is going to the butcher."
"Mr. Jones is going to the races."
"Tommy Jones is in bed with a very bad cold."

After graduation and armed with a certificate
I was offered a job in Oran,
and without being sure of what Oran was, I accepted.
I couldn't pay my rent. It was a case of starve,
or pick up and go.

(Oran is not to be confused with Iran, the country. Oran is Algeria's second city. Algeria is in North Africa, to the west, next to Morocco, with a view north over the Mediterranean. As a European, it is peculiar to look over the Mediterranean towards Europe—especially when you don't know what it is you are looking at. Oran is the town where Albert Camus set The Plague, 'La Peste' in French. Not a laugh throughout 600 existential pages. Heh-ho!)

Mr. and Mrs. Jones go on a trip to France.
At the airport they discover they've lost their passports.
Along with feckless, Mr. and Mrs. Jones are sexless.
Will they find their genitalia, along with their passports,
in a corner of the bedroom?
For a corner of a bedroom can embody resilience,
if it's out of view.

In Oran, I became friends with the owner of the school. Ali.
It was a mystery how Ali came to own the school—
for after winning the war against French colonialism,
Algeria was socialist, and private property
was taboo.
When Ali dived into the Mediterranean,
when he re-surfaced,
his *Afro* had the same symmetry
as when he'd disappeared underwater.
He embraced emancipation, of course.
Emancipation was also taboo.

Tommy Jones and his sister Susan Jones are lying on the beach.
Without bulges in their swimsuit shapes,
they have a gargantuan sense
of right and wrong. Mrs. Jones drinks tea.
Imprisoned in the book, she wants illicit friendships,
corrupt exchanges unattached to formal forms.

(After colonization by the Carthaginians, by the Romans, by Islamic hoards, by the Spanish and the French — the Algerians threw out the French in a war of Independence ending in 1962. During this war the Algerians put salt into the gaping wounds of Frenchmen and placed them in the mud flats. The French chucked living Algerians from helicopters into the Mediterranean blue.)

Let's study the conditional.
We are at the twins' 16th birthday party
(Did I mention that Tommy and Susan Jones are twins?)
on the grass outside their living room.

IF Mrs. Jones runs out of the picture,
WILL she run along the Mediterranean into the vineyards
to squash the Algerian grape under feet large as any man's?

IF Mr. Jones broke from his embryo,
WOULD he flash his innocence in an endroit
where grammar has no place at all?

IF Susan gets older,
WILL she distinguish purse from vagina?

IF Tom took the Arabic gardener into the bushes,
and this middle-aged gardener forgot his Viagra,
WOULD anything ensue?

Who Is Your Favorite Royal?

"Who is your favorite Royal?"
This question implies obeisance is a privilege.
Difficult to stomach unless
one is beguiled by the astonishing lack of sweat
in aristocratic underclothes.

Personally, I do have an answer. I've had contact with a Royal
at close quarters.
I served Prince Charles while I was working in *Harrods*.
There, what's not to be forgotten can be bought in bottles
and the obtaining of needless possessions prevails.

I was working in the chemist's department over Christmas.
Our wages were audacious.
Payday was a fingering of our anus
so we stole to have enough to pay the rent.

If the transaction was in cash
and they handed over the exact amount
instead of going to the cash register we slipped the money
into our loose pockets,
and on its requisitioning we were on a par, in terms of wealth
(its dubious acquisitioning)
with Lords, Ladies, Barons, Baronesses.

Constant customers: never more than a selection of appetites,
a bundle of foibles, slithers of the ordinary,
masquerading as mahogany.
Unless one believes Title says more,
and that Class is the final fact.

So frequent were the visits of the Titled that when Charles
came incognito
we were all aware of the presence of a Prince

whose birth into the broad world had to be accepted
like *bacon* which, whatever your opinion, continues to exist.

An elderly equerry approaches.
I am the oracle at the counter.
"Is this the department for hot water bottles?"
Charles, obviously anonymous among the pharmacy shelves,
tended by his secret service
(detectives full of non-sexual energy)
(non-sexual 'Lords in Waiting')
(and who the hell non-sexual else?)
moves forward to hear my answer to this missal
from the court.

"We have the usual rubber models in all colors,
a model in the shape of a tortoise,
expensive models in stone."
"We're giving hot water bottles for Xmas.
We'd like the regular model. Say—fifty."
On the sudden, a flurried conference.
The group around the Prince forms a scrum out of which
the Prince's voice expounds,
"Make it sixty. Hell to pay if anyone's left out."

"Sixty then. Send them to the Palace. Put it on account."
(Important customers have a *Harrods'* account.)
I ask, "What Palace?" "Buckingham," is his answer.
He has no idea he's prancing on the frieze
of a Royal Stuccoed Joke.

In cold damp climates a container (usually rubber)
is filled with hot water (a hot water 'bottle')
and then taken into bed.
This object is proletarian
and helps with the circulatory system of the poorer classes.
Feet are meant to be placed upon it,
though it can be placed on all bodily areas,
inducing ecstasies in individuals
who have quite satisfactory heating systems in their homes.

In a capitalist system jokes are unacceptable
though humor is all about.
Throughout *Harrods* I become famous as the sales clerk
who has sold Prince Charles sixty hot water bottles.
A Japanese shoplifter stops by to strike up a friendship.
As he flirts, he eyes the locked cabinet
containing high-priced perfumes.

When dealing with an abusive system, retaliation is in order.
De rigueur. A la mode.
Here comes Management.
I am being considered for promotion.
This fate gurgitates a phantom of myself
mingling as a cocktail with the overwrought establishment.

My achievement will be to tear at the roots of its grammar,
squelch the tubers of its prejudiced vocabulary
and, instead of joining in the aristocratic oratory,
let out a screech at its wincing verbs.

I Met Julia Childs

Jobs turn on the coin of convincing the unconvinced.
In the early eighties I had such a job
finding new students for a posh French cooking school
in Chelsea. With prospective students,
my instructions were not to deviate from
a text placed in front of me.
In the introduction to page 25,
classical technique was stressed.
But when we left my office, wandering
among tiles, glass, nails, sheetrock partitions, on a tour
of the presumed school premises —
the candidates couldn't find the classicism.
Searching for classicism there,
they wandered
in a mess.

The phone rang and it was a secretary. "Hello,
this is Julia Childs' secretary." For Julia Childs had heard
about this new cooking school in Chelsea,
and Julia Childs wanted to come to lunch.
The school was not the least bit ready.
But once the owner talked to Julia, there was no turning back.
There was to be a gourmet lunch,
to celebrate the idea of the school,
in a facility with the feel
of an isle — always abandoned, never to be inhabited —
on Wednesday after next.

To that arranged concrete corner, in came Julia,
her personal assistants, and husband with her,
to enjoy the concrete, and the concrete mixer,
and whatever the young chef concocted on the plates.
There was vaulting ambition around that circular table!
A great case was stated by the Owner Principal,
and by the chef from Strasbourg in France
who erected vast delights
as Julia made gentle sketches
between the marks engraved by others —
distinguishing real talent from weak ink.

Her revolving interest returned always
to her husband opposite.
A long way across the table, he was older, senile perhaps,
yet Julia made it known he was a great organizer, purveyor
and, surely, lover.
If he could give such pleasure,
we hoped there was a little of what was left of him, in us

I often quoted Julia (I called her Julia)
and had photos of myself with Julia, Julia with myself.
Thus we found students. More than the desired quota.
One became the most popular chef in North America, well,
I don't know about Canada,
but certainly in the United States.
I'd talk about the school restaurant
(for which the students would help create the menu)
insisting the *state-of-the-art* kitchen didn't mean
our deal was mere *technique*.
"Technique," (this was pure Julia) "must not intrude
on what is shopped for, chopped, sauced, eaten
in a sensual space."

Julia's husband *was* senile,
but she included him in all dimensions—
as she did me on subsequent occasions—
though she never knew who the hell I was.
There was a notion the school was functional,
which is not to say there weren't accidents,
cuts from kitchen knives deep enough for hospitals,
disagreements over a curriculum
with roots too deep in Haute Cuisine. After graduation,
a recession made it difficult for students to find positions,
and students were mocked in kitchens
for being Queer
or being Women.
A few in that first class were Queer men who died
in the first flush of AIDS.

Inevitably the Owner Principal satisfied her ambitions
to become a social titan.
The Student who was to become famous was already primed.
The Teacher Chef married the richest student,
later marrying women ever richer, of interesting cultures,

to erect new cuisines.
And Julia lived with rumors of alcoholic lesbianism,
of saving France from different revolutions,
of slipping a chicken back in the pot
after she had dropped it on the floor
in the early days of TV when there was little editing
on account of the unrelenting actuality
of the moment on screen.
Then Julia's husband didn't accompany her anymore.
He'd passed away.

But she had a mechanism for dealing with evolving matter
whether from too much boiling or too much soiling,
as bubbles exploded, occupying attention
before their journey, deep in the dish at the table's centre —
"It must be tasted! Mustn't it! Look at it!"
Appreciation is brother/sister to the transformation
bound to happen
when concord is produced and taste's sublime.

Hiding

Birth is a naked event
but a Queer Baby Boy
must be dressed.
Sharp on the heels of my very first breath
came the trip to the font.

We're talking Christenings. The necessary ablutions.
Relatives under ancestral influence
put me in an hereditary number
a long white gown
white embroidery encrusted
pure on pure.
Mind you, I knew how to wear it.
Carted to the church through the village street
I proudly languished
as my gown flowed.

A Red Fox brayed in the mid morning mist.
"That effeminate Babe is exquisitely dressed."
A Rook by the brook about to eat a Gnat cawed.
"I adore the extravagance of so many bows."

In certain regions of the earth
Naked Babes are totally immersed
in absurdity.

For adult sex
as an adult
I reverted to the naked state.
Yet before I stripped
I bowed to the taste of those
who on the fly
preferred bronze buttons to a zip.
Nice prospective perpetrators show interest in clothes.

My Funeral was muddled.
After my body
(shrunk to next to nothing)
was put in a craven suit
funeral purveyors undressed it
to concentrate on what would be everlastingly under—
my underclothes!
How butch, how brief, how femme, how silk
couldn't be ascertained
from open-hearted laughter
as the decision was reached
on the hue
to complement
my surprisingly strong bones.

Pretending

Thought I'd introduce myself with a descriptive fantasy.
If you find it appealing get in touch.
Let's see if we can see me see myself with the walk of, say,
Anouk Aimee.
Or better yet Arletty, the dame from *Les Enfants du Paradis* —
who, as she walked, didn't touch.
And neither do I as I enter the dimly lit bar
of the elegant hotel — eloquently, I don't touch.

And unmistakably there's no mistake,
my intoxicating body smell
washes over small areas and does it well —
one whiff of me bringing with me waves of the compound
of outside stuff.

And of course I'm wearing a skirt with a length that's short
and of the color black
and what should cover the upper portion of me
but a tight tight top
and there are sandals with the heel high
and the strappy strap that twines and twines
to the knee
oh it can't stop
and you with your massive intellect
(which you keep under control)
can't stop looking at the beauty of my old leg
with exquisite calve.

Aware that great distances abound and are always too close —
I walk in tall glory
in the near empty room till I sit on a stool not far away at all,
with all eyes in the near empty bar on my confidence,
complete,
not overstuffed.

As with a great surprising smile I glance in your direction,
the essential peripherals of your 6 ft 6 inch frame
in tense anticipation straighten.
And as you lean over

to grab the drink the bartender has left you
(because of course he knows you)
with originality you whisper,
for you are a true original,
"Could I offer Helen of Troy a sip?"

First you lean. And then without disguise that you are aching,
aching to be next to me, you change your seat.
Did I want you in closer? Did I already motion?

I whisper, "My nose is too big to be Helen of Troy.
Whatever it is that you are drinking,
that's the drink I'll drink."
You arch back to take in the legginess of me
which goes up and down both ways.
And I ask directly if the stare
which darts from your eyes with the famous flare
is the unalloyed stare of a stare at my newly pedicured feet.
You start making stupid excuses,
so I put my hand on your brain.
Uh! I meant to say your knee.

Because as a person with a very long past
and a couple of genders, I know
the effect I'm having. It's quite OK.

Do you want a closer look at the pedicure? I bend forward
ostensibly to cross over the legs.
And as for the panties,
did you get both primary and secondary looks in just those
several seconds of sequence executed
within the delicacies of this sway?
I ask if you want to feel the smoothness.
Unable to resist, you're leaning forward,
your naturally huge novice masculine hand
is stopping at the hem of my short skirt. You say,
"Smooth." I say, "I shave
every day."

Nothing has been exposed. In fact
you are looking down as drunks look
when they are imagining a light brush of their lips

behind the knee.
So I whisper, "Why has your hand stopped?"
And I take my hand, like fruit from a tree,
and I put it over yours—
and heat emanates from where we don't know
because really it's not about electricity travelling,
it's about nesting. My hand, and the top of my leg
with your hand between.

Then in a dominant well-shaped sentence
you ask if my little breasts are an invention
of a kind of extension. But it's only words.
The real story is the undercurl
of the majority of your fingertips
except one—which stretches in its girth.

In *Doctor Faustus*, Helen of Troy is on and off in minutes.
"Is this the ship?" —and she's vanished without an etcetera.
Also in *The Iliad*,
all things considered, she's hardly around.
But that's the beauty of it, for our necks go back as if hit
with a strong kiss
and in this pool of passion we try to taste
the wonderful 'thing' of her
and would, were we to realize that the wonderful 'it' of her
will remain unseen.

I Wish I Belonged To This Story

I wish I belonged to this story –
Anything from a piece of a character, to a mood...
Events begin when character number one
whose name is Steve
(Steve is Steve's real name) is fifteen years old
(it's a hell of a story) and Steve is watching a movie
in the cinema he's inherited in a conservative western town.
Steve is the projectionist, cashier, publicist, usher.
His girlfriend and friends help,
but there's a certain momentum when he does things on his own.

The week's film is *The Rocky Horror Picture Show*.
He projects one scene over and over with the cinema empty,
the conservative audience presumably gone home.
The cause of his captivation is a transsexual rock-rock-rocking.
Steve lays claim to the rocking of this transsexual.
This rocking transsexual in *The Rocky Horror* lays claim
to the boiling blood of the appropriate newness in his soul.

Steve's process continues with nails –
lacquered, grown to a length, then grown to a length beyond.
The conservative audience notices
as he gives them the tickets, "Have you seen Steve's nails?"
Faced with a green brighter than the faces on their dollars,
the customers go along with whatever hues Steve proffers.
I would love to be the blue suggestive mist,
the almond going on scarlet, these devastating hues...

Before you can say 'where's the varnish?' –
Steve has progressed to dressing as female characters
from the films. He is best at revivals.
For *Goldfinger* he imitates Shirley Bassey's delirious delivery
of the title song – with a loudspeaker – in golden clothes.
And as for accessories (it's all in the accessories)
his earrings have danglers dangling on the danglers.
The townsfolk go to the cinema more to bask in his costume
than in the show.
On the way home they sing *Goldfinger*,
throwing rationalism in the gutter.

I want to be a rodent living in that gutter,
devouring rationalism, dissolved by my acids,
mundanely excreted, irrationally exposed...

In adolescence Steve wears a padded bra
under his sweater. Then in adulthood,
in a neighboring metropolis,
a surgeon makes incisions just below the nipples
and in an hour has injected hard soft tissue—
so that Steve comes out
with titties lilting, yet perked as cones.
Steve's girlfriend has accompanied him,
deducing this evolution would be an added attraction.
She isn't wrong. "Heavens!
Steve's got titties and he's not advertising his cinema!"
But Steve has a talent for all things electrical.
With his breasts instead of a chest,
in a mini-skirt instead of jeans, he repairs
TVs Central Heating Systems Coolers
Lamp Disconnections Computers Radios DVDs.

Some are disconcerted because he does dress like a hooker.
Yet he is more Steve than ever,
with a comfort that substantiates itself in others—
which is the making of a politician.
So when he runs for Mayor, he wins.

A crowd appears from Kansas
to shout "This transsexual leader is an abomination!"
Though conservative, the townsfolk become so angry
that a percentage of husbands put on their wives' dresses,
while their wives dress in their husbands' dungarees,
and together they advance on the demonstrators
who are demonstrating against Dangerous Trangressions
by stamping on the flag of the USA.
I want to belong to this story, be the Flag, picked from the dust,
carefully folded, placed in Steve's hands
as the marauding insulters wither away...

2
PRIVATE VIEW

*So you dare conclude
Because my verse is wanton that I'm lewd?
Fools! Though the sacred poet should abjure
Grossness himself, his work need not be pure
Indeed it will taste dry and dull unless
It's sauced and slated with licentiousness
And has the power to tickle and provoke
Some action...*

— *Catullus*
(trans, James Mitchie)

Private View

In New York I holler.
I've torn up European roots and come out bedraggled.
In Britain, army-navy-air-force are being used
to keep dominion over The Falklands,
tiny South Atlantic Islands.
Skinheads beat up Pakis.
Conservatives wear tweeds.
So I've come across the pond to dance another imperial dance.
From the deep roots of my follicles
to the clear thrust of my cuticles
I must embody all the uniforms, wield the gaudy dream.

I become a WAITER.
Up on 41st, waging royal battles over profitable tables,
our conflagrations are inspired by Reagan and his Nancy —
Emperor and Empress of the Mighty Mean.

I become a REAL ESTATE BROKER.
A flabby gent who lives in Manhattan
in a sharp apartment on chicest 5th
has acquired a former factory space up in Yonkers.
My job is to sit in this unloved space
and phone a list of numbers.
"Hello. My name is John Marcus
and I've heard you are looking for 50,000 square feet."
I then read verbatim the typed scripted information
as to adaptability to
spectacular night club arts centre any variation of retreat —
over the screaming of the victim, "I'm not looking for nothing,
have never looked for anything except love and peace!"

I become a RECRUITER.
A recruiter's job in this trade school is to grab
the under-educated
and persuade them to enroll in
motor body motor repair welding air conditioning courses.
Motor body consists of bending out the bends.
Motor repair necessitates sympathy with wear and tear.
Welding is in the frizzing and sparking

as with two metallic pieces you are larking.
And if you air condition in summer, you can heat in winter
with the knack of turning the process round
the other bleeding way.

Didn't convince many.
Certain days, didn't convince any.

Didn't mind!
For from my screened-off office space,
outside the window picture-framing the street
during lunch hour,
I am visited by a Flasher.
As long as there are meetings with his monster,
who cares about Margaret Thatcher?
(If the necessary force had been sought through *my* aggression,
The Falklands would have been handed back
to the Argentinians
with raucous laughs, not rage.)

With a great deal of secondary staring,
I keep that Flasher guessing.
Am I recognizing his sausage as a length
of South American Candy pressed against the pane?
Or do I see it as a Transfer?
Remember Transfers? — gummed paper,
four times the size of postal stamps,
to be peeled out of comic books,
then pressed onto forearms.
No matter how delicately we transfer the Transfer
onto our inexperienced bodies,
the colors run, contours seeking out other boundaries,
leaving us with our own square of smudged romance —
a mix of hot blood ink English tea and cream.

Muscled Mounties

We are staying in a chalet on the Olympic Peninsula
with a view over the Straights of Juan De Fuca
to Vancouver Island.
Vancouver Island veers towards the Arctic,
but in confrontation across this water
is a west/east, east/west, longitudinal eyeball stretch.

My inexpensive binoculars
make out perimeters, outlines of ranges.
My friend's expensive binoculars
delineate bays with boats, glacial valleys,
tropical birds which, mistaking the continent,
sport incongruous plumes.

Later, not moving from the living room,
viewing through the window, he shouts,
"Whales!" — in the accidental sea, across the immediate lawn.
My binoculars register stretches of water weed known as kelp.
And where my friend is certain
he's seen a cub with its mother,
I have an unblocked view of an indigent patch of rock.

Anyway, tonight we're due for a most dramatic
meteor shower. My friend reaches the conclusion
that this meteor shower is the reason we've come.

OK, I'm a pessimist. But all I'm likely to witness is a candle
at some withered carnival.
He'll see fiery tails soaring,
while my lights will be apparitional.
My ego is already an artificial blossom on a paper stem.

Mind you, over on Vancouver Island,
among peaks bigger than Everest,
is the exact same setting of our favorite porno film
in which Canadian Mounties
are lured by Canadian Hunks
into Canadian Huts
where they stay, because snow hard as their erections

has piled up for months.

I grab my friend's binoculars and let him know
they are in the act of filming a sequel.
Will the Mounties leave the Canadian Hunks
at the inexorable melt, or stay to enjoy
the next inevitable snow?

A Canadian Mountie on the mountain takes off his jock strap
and throws it across to his Mountie friend
on the opposite range.
(I return my friend's binoculars.)
"You didn't see it? What a pity. It was the last shot.
They've packed up.
They did it so professionally —
it won't be necessary for them to do it again."

Master Of The Hurricane

On Saturday a force of nature
buys an iced tea in MacDonald's.
He is a perfect 21 year old.
With his fecund muscle
and dangling dangler
he is the sweet proportion of a disaster.
He is a natural complexity aching to sing its song.

Physical perfection is pervasive and, in Playboy style,
has vulgarities.
This fleshed personification of nature's taste, however,
is the brutal opposite of banal.
After he's finished his beverage he will be transmuted
above New York City
to become Master of the Hurricane.
The architecture of his shoulders
will protect the bolstering phantom blizzard.
His capacious head, lovingly particularized,
topped by dreadlocks of lacy hemlock
will be the centre of the storm.

While he's ordering his iced tea
Mayor Bloomberg with fashionable Politicians
happens to pay a visit to MacDonald's —
and they are all traumatized by the bulge of his package
which betrays the constant requisitioning of his conscience
and makes them feel alone.

Dear God, his sincerity is so extravagant, the politicians
are flummoxed.
When this super-animal cradles his cup of iced tea
in hands indicative of all points of the compass,
the Mayor and the Politicians crowd the counter.
"We want an iced tea too!" they scream.

Mayor and Politicians watch as he exits MacDonald's.
The whole political caboodle considers following him
down into the subway.
But the subways are not running —

so he ascends into the airways,
for as Master of the Hurricane he has to do his job
to demonstrate he's been born.

The Mayor is no dummy (as he tells us consistently).
Taking a gander at the young man's ass
as it is pulled clear of the earth's mass,
he considers it a shelf for radical idling,
a platform for the performance of revolutionary songs.

Cameras crowd into MacDonald's
as the Mayor gives a speech, elucidating
the difference between pros and cons.
"Don't be taken in," he instructs.
"This pre-storm calm is nothing but hypocrisy."

"Expect calamities. Manhattan sinking. Tornadoes ripping.
Innocent throats slashed with smashed glass,
perpetrated by a vigor that needs to harm."

Above the city, the Master of the Hurricane
lets his breath lie latent in the magnificence of his chest.
If he breathes out, the Metropolis will be obliterated —
to be inevitably reconstituted (but not for long).

Inside or outside time (unrecognized if it's not measured)
he'll return! With fire flaring
from his blow torch tits, he'll burn to bits
institutions, comfort, variegated individuals —
by licks from his leathery tongue.

Now this is not orgasmic. Orgasmic is for the tragic.
Them that so desires will be allowed to kneel
to kiss the cock ring
anointing his sacred dong.

Trip To Paradise

A friend buys a DVD on a street in Guatemala.
The vendor tells him, "This is a DVD unlike any other.
Prepare!"

But can there be preparation for fellatio performed
by an athletic South American male

on the generous genitalia of a good-looking Stallion? —
both South American and Stallion
products of an amorous soil, its gift.

How to prepare
for horse ecstasy in a corner of the jungle?
For sharp sympathy between participant and viewer
in or out of frame?

The massive animal hardly moves, doesn't neigh.
Tantalization induces inner moaning,
interior thinking,
silent screams.

*

A man in the Pacific Northwest dies
from intimacy with a stallion?
The stallion, in guiltless abandon,
ruptured the man's colon.

*

On a clear day outside Seattle
Mt Rainier (a volcano) stirs in atmospheric stupefaction.

Among clouds, mists — the peak is hidden
till the raw volcano rears its presence,
snow-smeared in summertime.

At the base of the volcano, men and horses
are about to commune, to romantically liaise.

The Stallions wait in the anticipatory stables
as the humans, in a friendly group, imbibe alcohol or tea.

Here trees are monstrous and defy designation.
Foreground and background interweave
in multitudinous greens.

Grass pushes up in thirsty bundles.
This is where lava flowed and will flow again.

After the conflagration
with passion keen

the man
—riding the Stallion that killed him—

trots up to paradise,
the highest village below the snow-line.

Wandering along paths
through meadowlands of flowers,

the horse trots attentively
so as not to molest the blossoms,

and is astonished to be ridden by this Spirit
who steers by teasings of the tousled mane.

*

Strolling towards them,
citizens meditate on the propensities
of an active volcano on an afternoon of a weekend day.

They are mightily jolted
as the Stallion passes on the narrow path—
the ghost rider can be seen.

They frantically deny all knowledge of the Spirit.
For even a glimpse entails
the year-in year-out wearing
of castigated necklaces.

Secret piercings
necessitate monstrous jewels
in private places.

Like it or not they must bear
the transgressive burden of the beads of play.

Tenant Patrol

        I live on the ninth floor of a New York City Project
        and my guests are vetted. In the lobby
        they sign a red leather-bound book.
        This signature is the stamp of their Persona,
        affixed alongside the record of who they stayed with,
        their visit's duration, whether it occurred by night or day.
        If a guest enters or exits between 9pm and 5am,
        a security man is on duty
        and there's no confrontation.
        This security man views morality as intangible.
        No mind altering answers
        to unanswerable questions.
        No integration of rules
        when unrecognizable games are played.

But daylight hours are another story.
From 7am to early evening,
a Tenant Patrol, consisting of a dozen or so *ordinary* tenants,
sits in the lobby,
checking who likes what in what positions.
We're talking Chinese Bullies, Mafia Papis, Wannabe-Rabbis,
New England Mother Superiors—whose sole credential
is that they live in the building.
A visit is a psychosis which buckles the duct of the normal,
tears a vent.
Knowledge is ascertained
by evidence visitors are not privy to—
how the spidery genital on the stairwell casts its shadow
as they sign their name.

        My guests are varied
        and when we come together, hopefully
        it's shocking. Where there's shock,
        there's breath! But oftentimes
        we discuss food
        (in a stew do you use canned broth?)

or the latest movie
(how it curls around its breadth).
Whoever the visitor—
Susan Sontag
Mick Jagger
Madonna
Phillip Roth
Hustling Porn Star
Keats
(we are discussing my social life
in the reality of dreams)—
whoever comes round after breakfast
in a ninth floor bedroom
of a twenty story building
of a New York City Housing Project,
both I and the guest end up huddled in the trenches,
strategizing the meeting with the looming Patrol—
how we'll muster our defenses.

I wish I had the courage of the hooker staying with the guy
(who disclaims her) up on the fourteenth or maybe the tenth.
She stays with this guy and she says she's his daughter.
She isn't his daughter. She's a hooker—
part truck driver, part Medusa,
part Queen Mab who queens the night.
When she comes in with a client, the Tenant Patrol screams,
"You don't live here! You don't have rights!"
She brandishes the finger
and, encouraging her client, passes without signing.
No feigned humility
disguises the supremacy of her entrance into the elevator
(her flower garden)
where one plus one equals forty-two
when you appreciate the scent.

Tenant Patrol *Redux*

I live alone in a one bedroom apartment
on the 9th floor of a 20 story New York City building—
and when I saw Rudy's photo on Craig's List,
advertising his services
at a sensible price,
I phoned and he came over and spent the night.
One o'clock, we go up to the roof
where the shy dark symphony that is the city below
marches to a distant marching band.

At the other end of the spectrum, on the ground floor
where gravity is an affliction,
the Tenant Patrol (those tenants with extraordinary wisdoms)
sits in the lobby from dawn to dusk
insisting, with authority, that guests sign their names
in the book of morality.
Morality was not inaugurated a priori, but later,
with the animate dinosaurs and chewing gum,
boy scouts and polar bears,
who helplessly embody the age of shame and fright.

When we emerge from my apartment in the morning
after sorting our underclothes
which were entwined like boys in play
I direct Rudy towards the stairs with EXIT blazoning,
and away from the elevators that descend to the lobby.
He's getting on. And I am older. As old soldiers
we don't need censorship at the border—
a reasoning that, in its right to question, is obscene.

We open the fire-door to the stairwell, walk down eight floors
to the second story
where we open another fire-door to the street. If these doors
are pushed brutally, their sirens don't respond. Brutality
calls forth a mysterious intelligence
which, if it could reconcile the equation of me running away
from what I'm not afraid of,
would be just neat.

Outside, in preparation for stairs going down to a garden,
we're on a Mussolini landing with Mussolini railings.
Beyond the rail, through branches without leaves,
the early street is ready to transform
to mesmerizing scenes.
If I had it in me (I do have it in me!) I'd give a speech
strong as the hate than Mussolini's,
one in praise of the discovery of the genders in me, of sex
in middle early to the middling early aging aged.
I'd deliver a poem up to the windows of the rear apartments —
in Puerto Rican Guatemalan Spanish Mandarin Cuban
Haitian French Brooklyn Bostonian English
with rhymes of Vietnamese.
"I'm down here! " I'd sing out. "Down here
where the serpentine route dictates a serpentine course!
Down here! With a new hustler, Rudy!
I'm wild about Rudy! Rudy's wild
about his English Queen!"

Summers in New York City

Sustaining the summer scorcher
is the acquired act of the New Yorker.
The attire for now (what will it be to come?)
is an itsy t-shirt with a sluggy low slung jean
framing that unmanageable playing field —

                                         the blatant bum.

Arses from everywhere (with their complexity of the human,
not of the machine)
are meant to be looked at face to face.
The environs of the tantalizing crack above the low slung jean
exhibit changes as changeable and unchangeable
as at the beach.
The tide that was a while ago, now isn't —
but still reaches the shore just fine.

Swinging septuagenarian sloops,
ambivalent ambidextrous hoops,
conservative cracks, liberal smacks,
are pointed out by guides from the tops of buses.

Our guides (guardians of New York's constitution)
are nothing but Marxist Populist when handling information
in 90 degree humidity, passing this secret on as consolation:
"The ordinary terrace table is the best position
to appreciate the urban wobble."

New York offers pleasures in dimension,
but nothing betters the superficial.
The repetition of the trivial
renders superficial into monumental. It's divine.

Prevailing Sensations

1
Two summers ago I sat on this bench
with the glare of the sun right upon me.
This bench was one bench among many. The rest were empty.

> — When this guy came over to sit absolutely next to me
> in the tradition of one character talking to another
> in a play.

He talked of his enormous package
and the prevailing sensation was
that he was speaking of a work that had delighted the critics.

> Critics had coalesced over the fine details
> and when they'd got round to the central impulse
> compliments had rained.

His coda was: "This thing between my legs
has such a desire to be looked at.
Let's meet in fifteen minutes in MacDonald's."
(We checked our watches.)
"At the moment something else is playing on my mind."

> I never had the opportunity to size up the matter.
> I waited in Macdonald's, went the next day,
> waited again,
> but there was no sign of him.

2
He didn't put in an appearance at the benches
the rest of that summer,
or the next winter, or during the course of the year.

> Through all seasons I carried a tape measure, to check
> whether his version of wide was my version of wide,
> whether we had the same vision of the length of long.

.

This park has roads
along its southern bottom, and its topmost northern.
Side-roads cut cross and divide it into oblongs.
These oblongs are miserable tarmac patches
when nothing's going on,
but happily there's usually basketball in the top oblong,
football in the middle oblong,
and the bottom oblong has the Senior Center.
Behind the Senior Center, these fifteen benches—
where space is limited,
time is endless,
and an isolated arrangement of plants and trees implies
that this is a place where companionship may not belong.

> Yet what is ascertainable is that eventually
> something *has* to happen.
> The benches are arranged in a semi-circle,
> in the expectancy of action,
> and the non-communicating trees and plants
> stand waiting for—?
> A sex show? A symphonic song?

3

This summer, he finally reappeared—but didn't recognize me.
After flirting with the ladies who eat at the Center,
he sat down to repeat the details of his enormous dong.

> Then he added:
> "My three piece set has a desire to be looked at.
> Meet me at Macdonald's. Later.
> Momentarily I have something that must be done."

Over a solitary burger I ascertained that in Macdonald's
I corresponded to the shape of a character
in the yet-to-be-completed enormity
of the globe's psycho-sexual plan.

Jane's Husband

Jealousy
was the name of my friend Jane's husband.
I was sharing an apartment with Jane in New York City
when she'd met him.
To be with him, she moved out.

She liked older men, yet he was fifteen years younger;
good looking, when she preferred character;
slim, when she enjoyed the security of stout.

He was so jealous he could only stare at me.
It made no difference that Jane and I were brotherly/sisterly,
that I was Queer. His naked jealousy
looked like an exposed hard-on.
He was infatuated with his own doubts.

They married and moved to a house
outside a village outside Manhattan.
The only humans around who might cause problems
were shapes passing the other side of a thick privet hedge
along a lonely road.

*

A message arrived from England.
Would Jane come over to look after her mother
who was in a deathly state?
Jane went. Hubby went with her. But her mother survived,
her demise extended.
Weeks made friends with months, months married the years,
years were like the holes in clothes,
breaking out into an opening, no sign of the finish
that delineated an end.

*

Jane's mother's house
was isolated
and through a window was a view of a field
at the bottom of a garden of great length.

Over the fence an obese farm-laborer
tended unattractive cows.
Jane's husband was therefore happy —
until one day, rummaging among Jane's possessions,
he discovered
two wigs.

Jane insisted she intended to wear them one day.
They'd incarnate a new image.
Furthermore they were part of her privacy. *Her* privacy!
They were not his!

He didn't argue.
It was simple: these wigs proved
that in New York City
Jane had traveled in disguise to where the giant-genitaled live.

*

I return from a business trip.

The light on my answering machine tells me there is message
after message.
It is Jane's husband. He is in America, up at the house,
checking the privet hedge.
Before he returns to Jane in England, he needs to see me.

After mumbling a greeting, he sits down
and with great sincerity
delves in the box he is carrying
and on the table
places the two wigs.

He tells me to make no attempt to deny
I had educated Jane in perversity.
Was it in Paris that her education began?

True, Jane and I had met in Paris.
And he must have heard my story
of the naked hookers who danced in car headlights
in the middle of the night
in the middle of the Bois de Boulogne.
A friend had taken me on a drive to show me.
But as we watched, the hookers were already in the act
of disappearing.
We'd scanned the outskirts of a wood,
but saw no trace of where they'd gone.

*

The sharp shrill of pleasure
is said to be better
when you don't understand what you do.

I try on the blond wig and my blood runs quicker.
Jane's husband tries on the black wig
and the whole of him shivers.

We are thrashing bulldogs on the shore of his suspicions
in a land where silhouettes are strong.

Disposables

Pushing a supermarket chariot,
he is fearless. On the look-out for disposables,
he is disposing. He is rangy homeless.
What passes between us
is a *let's-go-in-for-secrecy-more-or-less-immediately* impact gaze.

"Change please. I'm looking for food."
I give him 20 bucks.
"Is this a note? What are you after?
                                         Ahh, you're lucky.
I can be ever so kind if I don't feel fooled —
and I know a place."

Away he starts and I follow. I'm holding a briefcase
because a Japanese woman has asked me
to teach her son English,
and I've just come from the first lesson with this eight year old
who picks up grammar intonation quick as a hint,
knows English is a waterfall to run under,
laughing and suffocating — his enjoyment's immense.

He holds my twenty very respectfully.
Money is used to frighten off animals in the night.
Anyway, he's walking. And as he's walking he relates.
"At the weekends I find myself with expensive women.
They cost in the region of hundreds of dollars — which I pay
to experience myself not as your average flibberty-jibbit,
but as a grown-up guy."

He beckons me into the doorway of an active garage.
I simulate being affronted. This he refuses to believe.
"But this is an active garage!" — straight to his face I tell him.
He tells me — "I'll put you in my supermarket chariot.
It'll be your spot. I'll keep you in it for days."
His humor is a gift far beyond the question
of money to be exchanged.

At Delancey he stops in an alcove formed
at the edge of a construction site.

I tell him — "This isn't a place.
This is close to passenger vehicles, baby strollers, SUVs."
"Noooo!"
He gives instructions —
"What you must do is walk to the junction,
then come back behaving as if you are normal,
and I will deliver a fine urination. You'll see."

I go to the junction.
On my return the stream coming out of him is limited chaos
amid social hygiene, hygiene too clean.
Nobody gets hurt.
He gets 20 dollars and, from a distance,
I obtain a glimpse of a ferocious spurt
in the lazy dying of the day.
Compared with political crimes all over the planet,
it's an OK perversion.
You must agree.

Casual Public Exhibitionist

Public exhibitionist
        ex-militia
a healthy variety of marine
        working in Manhattan
living in Queens
        reliable, readily, radically able
in the boiling pot called havoc
        the curdling cream

Forty five years two months and a day
        by a Gillette razor
squeakyclean
        forever reliable radically able
he's clean he's cream

Casually out
        public and about
takes you to the element of extremes
        cream curdled
flesh colored lycra tights
        non see through
but you'll think you see through
        boiled in the pot called havoc
he's come out cream
        he's cream

Flesh colored non see thru lycra tights
        cold gear turtleneck mock
is a short black one
        cut above the waist
and the general public thinks
        he's coming from a gym
there is no gym
        just his clear outline
non dependent on a seasoned time
        it's his

not yours not mine
        it's cream

Came back with it
        miraculously intact
from the heated quarters of a tank
        to wear his
one piece zippered front
        skin colored short sleeve
biketard
        skin tight attached to bike shorts
which have the chiseled outline
        of low hanging balls
they're his
        not yours not mine

General public believes he's biking
        to and from the gym
there is no bike
        thinking of absence of gym absence of bike
arouses an excitement that comes from being bright
        he's bright

He was in tanks
        and he was in jeeps
and in his brand new above the waist
        fishnet mesh short sleeve top
his well developed top
        is seen living in a cage
he possesses this cage
        look at him caged

With a casual boldness he'll go to the mall
        in his rip stop transparent short shorts
with the same top
        worn over his barely covered
front pouch bikini with the open back
        exposing his ass in the great gentle rain

And the general public whispers
        the guy doesn't realize the see through is total
doesn't realize wind whips side splits
        of upward flaps of running shorts unlined
the material is lycra and the splits
        go right up right up so we're no longer thinking
of the gentle rain.

Emails

Dave was addicted to the computer.
He sent me an email with attachment
before he died.
"Look at this photo!
This is Rocky."
The photo was of a male nude, nearing 50.

"After I pass away Rocky will contact you.
He'll restore your *joie de vivre*."

Dave dies.
Emails from all over sympathize.
As a thank-you, I reply with the email of Rocky's photo—
as an elegy to my life with Dave.
Rocky's image bounds
to Europe, Africa, the West Coast,
as Dave's coffin descends into the grave.

"Wow!" emails a philosopher in Paris.
"*This* is a body. I love the thighs."

An acquaintance in Seattle
emails that this alarming charmer
will take me to areas
where the underneaths do rattle.
(Pacific Northwest eroticism
is seismic not biological.)
(A more biological high would be a whale displaying
a vivid water spout in the bay.)

Rocky emails.
His street smarts are delectable.
He discusses flirtations and their positions.
And he understands I'm wise.
Not after money,
he'd like me to take him shopping.
What he loves are shopping malls.

I'll be tall, in my seventies.

He'll wear a hoody and be going on fifty.
I'm to wait at the F line turnstile—
1st Avenue entrance is the designated entrance,
2nd Avenue station the designated station,
Sunday between 6 and 6:30 the designated time.

He doesn't show.

At that turnstile I am rolling in turmoil.
News of this ass-shaking wallop
was to be digitally delivered
unto Paris, Seattle,
Tangier in Morocco,
Merida in Mexico.

And will still be.

I'll prove I belong to the big time—
emailing
the manifold immoralities
that followed on our non-meeting at the subway gates,
immoralities
far surpassing the politics of inbred states.

At the computer I'll mold as I wanna!
With Rocky as my stallion,
we'll make the emails quake!
Wheeled in my wheel chair to the digital spot,
Rocky and I will not stop
till there are no more wheels!

Searching 4 Str8 Bi Married Tops On The DL

This is a consensual matter
between 2 men / discretion / between the walls
it stays within.
What I'm looking for I'll clearly state.
[Do not respond if you're not looking to meet off line
face 2 face.]

I do not fuck pussy.
Nor do I chill with men that act pussy.
Back in the days we said 'sissy'.
We're talking femme-feminine.
Measure sex pragmatically—
Is it lively?
Is it dirty?
Is it free?
Please note what's said here completely,
so there are no issues / bullshit / games /
you being turned around at the door.
[I'm giving you full warning here.]

To any of the following I express no interest.
No STDs. No HIVs.
No males who are white
who want to know what I did last night
where the hell I've been.
No females. No transsexuals. No homo thuggettes.
No openly gays.
No escort hustlers. No versatile mongers.
No kissers, no scatters, no pissers.
No checker uppers. No stimulant bruisers.
No heavy drug users.
[Drinks are cool, a modicum of weed.]

Me / male / 30 / 190 / I've got over 11 inches.
[Thick.]
Into clean ass licking / licking then dicking.
American English only spoken language.

Don't spout any other.
[Single words are OK.]

If there's enjoyment
there'll be a return engagement. No Strings Attached. NSA.

Looking only for utmost discretion / in a naturally masculine / discreet / life bi-sexual /a hundred per cent straight married top / loving safe sex on the down low / no public display / with the proviso that the desired be quite other.
[Don't want a male that's too much like me.]

You're a male who in public gives no clue
you lust after your brothers
and the lust in you turns to looking after our troubles
cos you're a street smart / smart dawg /
wise / mature minded / brief boxer wearing / man's man.
[Hygienic hygiene.]

Times are weekends and evenings.
You'll be given directions.
If you're a vain muscle body-fanatic, it's a plus not a problem.
[If you look younger, I'll go older than 30.]
[As long as you're butch, I'll go down to 18.]

Showroom

'Sexual decorum' writ by laws
floating above / around the page
is at odds with technology
(they fight powerfully / gently).
The conundrum is —
when prohibited desire is manifested digitally,
the romantic heart is titillated.
This titillation is *Essential / Central*.
Central as opposed to *Superficial*.
Superficial is tassels on a fringe.

Latterly, the media has bemoaned the peril posed
by the website *Backpage.com*.
Consumers searching for a virginal apartment
a Christian towel rack
an ethical selection of jellies / jams
come across hustlers (escorts) / hookers (strippers)
who've established this new home-base after being banished
from other affronted parts.

The media, determined to prove its affiliation with innocence,
has forged
a premise —
"ONCE DESIRE IS ERASED IN ONE AREA
IT TURNS UP IN ANOTHER."
As if this wasn't known before they sat down at the computer,
before their grandparents put biros to paper.
As soon as one animal conceived another
in the Great Raw Naked,
this has been the fashion of the world's turn.

On my computer,
photos of hustlers (heroic) / hookers (bodacious)
are on the right.
I am sitting at a desk, making a selection, changing opinions.
(The photos would be stage left

if I belonged to the digital world
inside the screen.)
Across from the photos
age color height weight price
are listed along with promises of large surprises.
These lists have the geometry of poems.
Poems stimulate with large small truths / small big lies.

I flick through ads selling intelligent abdominals,
masculine projectiles, mammalian wiles
and settle on
"150 DOLLARS WILL PERMIT YOU TO PLAY
WITH MY LONG BLACK SNAKE."
I dial the number and am confronted with a gruff bass voice.
"Black snake! What are you talking about?
I'm selling furniture.
Can I interest you in some Queen Anne?
Come on!
I've not sold a piece for weeks!"

As an antique dealer his voice resonates with inevitable aging.
I accept an invitation to examine what he's got —
before it fades away.
What he shows me is desirable
("Behold," he intones. "Do you like what you see?")
and rare
(illuminated in the moment)
and under such conditions we steer beyond the outer spectacle
to touch deeper notions of display.
Then and there we loiter through his showroom,
developing a connection
founded on each other's love of craftsmanship,
on one another's interpretation of decay.

Smile

The Jamaican and myself have sexy get-togethers without previous arrangement. His name is *Smile*, and *Smile* collects used containers. His territory is lower Manhattan. All over lower Manhattan he pushes a shopping-cart piled high with empty cans.

Naked to the waist in hot weather, bandannaed, black muscled shiny, bulges delineated, on his way up to Avenue A to the machine that give 5 cents for every empty, he's John the Baptist, crying in the wilderness, "If you've got the time, Man—I can park the cart."

Meaning—after I give him 20 dollars, he'll chain his cart to a post and we'll whip into the video store where he'll thrust his Jamaican dimension through one of the last New York Glory Holes (as genuine a glory hole as any of the originals). This is high communion. From his chalice, *Smile* proffers his blood and flesh. My mouth is the Chapel of articulation. Full articulation of what me and *Smile* experience is available upon request.

What is thought on these occasions? Speaking for myself—the excitement of *Smile* being apostolic, his name being *Smile*, with his two front teeth missing in the enamel of an otherwise perfect set.

Speaking for *Smile*—he repeats GOOD GOOD GOOD GOOD GOOD on the other side of the hole. Though there is really nothing other-sided about glory holes. "ON THE EIGHTH DAY THE GOOD LORD CREATED THEM TO CONNECT—"

GOOD GOOD GOOD GOOD GOOD has the quality of the Bach cantata, "Sheep May Safely Graze". When *Smile* reaches the maximum ecstatic he is Johann Sebastian Bach incarnate. GOOD GOOD GOOD GOOD GOOD is the universal animate, with no sense of 'Lucky me' versus 'The Unfortunate Rest'.

Thus it was appalling when a friend of *Smile*'s (I was looking for *Smile* at the 5 cent machine on Avenue A) told me, "You know *Smile*. They killed him in jail. He's dead."

I imagined *Smile* in the state of martyrdom. Stabbed to buggery. Shot in the eyeball. Appendages wrenched. These visions reeled all the way from *Genesis* to *Revelations*—revelations revealed when I saw him two days ago in the street.

"I can park the cart—if you've got the time."

"*Smile*! Didn't they murder you in jail? Aren't you dead?"

"I ain't dead, man. I went to Florida."

"Florida and death! They're very similar!"

How to celebrate his resurrection? —I pass him twenty bucks and we go our separate ways. This abstinence is achieved by way of piety, in the certainty that the Glory Hole (an altar in an isolated quarry) anticipates our arrival. We'll approach with the tread of Saints.

My Abode

Let's face it, we have to be careful
about whom we take back home.

After an initial conversation the person I'm attracted to
turns out to be educated—

history, philosophy, comparative religion.
At the same time I have suspicions...

there is my ingrained understanding
of the murderous impulse,

of strategies for hostage taking,
of rituals involved in houses of ill repute.

The café where we've met has green surfaces,
giving the aspect of a room for competitions.

(Who is competing with—who is competing against—
who is competing for—whom?)

When I get up he automatically follows. Walking together,
we get an inkling of how one and the other of us endure.

He is looking for a Daddy. He has a military background.
I learned to shoot at school.

His long hair springing from an electric nest
is perfect energy.

(Conversely it conjures a longing for hair so short
it barely covers up the bone.)

In the tattoo on his forearm are Roots Deracinated,
twining an Earth which can't calm down.

(Conversely, how long till this design
impacts like purest corn.)

His sprite elegance implies an erotic intelligence
capable of turbulent inventions.

(Conversely, oh God! Exhaustion
practiced till the naked dawn.)

I could say, "Sorry . . . I'm too old anyway."
But there's boredom about honesty,

flat disappointment about dishonesty.
(I'm being attacked by the whole damn throng.)

What I'm ashamed of is that the subversive streak
I am so proud of—longs, minute by minute, to conform.

I lie, in a voice which contains an essence of me.
I say that I share my apartment with a Freak, who's straight.

I am obliged to go ahead, to plead my case.
Will he wait? He smiles the promise of the Goat God Pan.

As a man of honor I add, "I won't be long."
And I cross the road to enter a pretentious building,

one with a side exit. From there I beat it to my apartment,
empty, 10 blocks distant, up in the elevator.

I reach the seclusion
of my bleeding fortress.

Like the Lady of Shallot
if circumstances fit my agenda, I might come down.

3
NATURE OF QUESTIONS

*The sins threw them back upon the steps,
And forced them to look for other places;
For their demons can only stay where charity is sure.*

— *Rimbaud*
(trans, Louise Varese)

Nature Of Questions

Questions proliferate.
I'll go as *a priori* as I can manage —
"Do I have to leave?"
"Is the exterior nothing more than Tryst after Tryst?"
These were my concerns as I lounged inside Mam's belly.
Also — *"If this womb is inside my Mammy,
what is my Mammy inside?"*

Later, much later, on my way to a plutocratic meeting,
as I walk —
questions are expected.
I ask the bright noon sky,
"Why don't clouds descend to halo me, stole me, shroud me?"
Down below, my tootsies ask the sidewalk,
*"What is the British equivalent for sidewalk?
Path? Walkway? Paved Ground?"*

In an office on Christopher Street
I supply answers to a technocrat.
We are hidden behind his plastic carbon screen.
This is an annual meeting, and this financial-aid officer
negotiates the paperwork necessary
for me to renew my participation in Medicaid.
Medicaid is medical insurance for those
with multiple medical conditions
and no income — paid by the country, the state.

To renew Medicaid it is preferable
to respond to the Inquisitor in a tortured fashion.

RENT.................................*"Why don't I own?"*
                              "Am I a commie?"

MARRIAGE........................*"Do I view it as inconvenient
                              to be someone else's property?"*
                              *"Was I divorced because
                              I couldn't get it up?"*
                              "Didn't I sometimes get it up?"
                              "Could I not get it up

> *because of confrontation*
> *with the same old same?"*
> *"In marriage*
> *between all kinds of genders*
> *isn't this a constant?"*
> *"Is constant synonymous with*
> *always always to remain?"*

The financial-aid officer, judging by his hairstyle,
must be heterosexual.
That dark clump, stuck to his skull, is pleased raw pain.

GREEN CARD....................*"Am I a non-citizen because patriotism*
is akin to fascism?"
"Is the Pope the Generalissimo?"

AND HERE'S A TOPIC.....*"What's my faith?"*

THEN THE GOB STOPPER WHEREIN THE QUESTIONER IS
INTERROGATOR SUPREME.....

> *"What have I done to deserve*
> *another period of survival?"*
>
> *"Period of survival?!"*
> *"Survival! Period!"*
>
> You say, *"Tomarto."*
> I say, *"Tomayto."*
>
> You say, *"AIDS."*
> I say, *"HIV."*

Things are quiet in his office.
"If I don't get on the program, what'll happen?"
The price of medication is high on the mountain,
the shack at the bottom is my total means.

By the way—if I ask, *"What is uncertainty?*
—Is that postulation or question?"
Depending on inflection postulation fades into question.
But the difference is not erased.
Always this agony between 'almost different'

and 'nearly the same'.

With the meeting over
I saunter a corridor
descend a stair
to a toted anonymity.

"If I proceed with anonymity...?"
Damn! Another question!
*"If I proceed in anonymity
die in anonymity
will the beat just beat?"*

If A Boyfriend Comes In With New Pants

If a boyfriend comes in with new pants
am I supposed to say? — "They're for a man 20 years younger."
Somebody at work asks me to dinner.
"No thanks, I don't like you. I have friends enough."
Essential honesty is a contract for disaster
and not a civilized response.
But there are levels.
It's a good idea to live halfway up the building.
On the roof you get soaked with lies.
In the basement, near the boiler, parched from truth.

I got a phone call from a good friend —
"That man is asking for your number."
My friend was talking of a thirty-or-so year old guy
I'd conversed with at a party.
I pass on my number. Mr. Thirty-Or-So rings me up,
we go out,
and he brings out ideas in the ancient part of me
that are slick and young and tough.
Two weeks into our relations he mentions,
"Eh, that girl you met me with at the party?
I got her pregnant.
Could you give me the necessary cash to call it off?"
Yeah, if the girl will consult a doctor friend of mine
with a clinic near Central Park.

But nobody appears outside the clinic,
though arrangements were specific.
It was all a fabrication.
I was supposed to hand over the cash he'd asked for
mano a mano — he's Italian — hand to hand.
He'd given a false address. As for the girl,
she didn't really know him.
And by that time he'd returned to Europe.
Did he need the money just for the money?
We never met to sort it out.
I was on a long list of fleeced fools called lovers.
My friend who gave the party says there were many
and that *should* help.

Mr. Thirty-Or-So makes no distinctions.
Both in Europe and America,
all ages and genders are treated to his pounce.

Is there something in his brain that makes him do it?
Information is processed just behind the forehead.
We have grey matter and white matter.
Grey matter by reputation enjoys sitting still, and being.
White matter is what moves thoughts to other thoughts,
it's the movement of the intelligence along.
With *too* much white matter *he* might connect with connections
all too quickly,
there'd be no time for analysis,
or for any wish to develop analytical ability.
An abstraction such as affection would be misconstrued.

With lies uncovered,
both deceiver and deceived live without shelter.
Is there no sign of a mist
that will cover all there is
and soothe my eyes?
The answer
is not to suck from a group of facts called *situations*,
to realize that similar facts
in different places
mutate to definitions we don't own.
This is known as *wisdom*—which, if you're old,
can be acquired at any age.

Incident On The Roof, 2001

First news of the Twin Tower disaster
was a radio announcement.
"An object seems to have collided – "
dilly-dallying to *" – a helicopter has gone in."*

There was an excellent view of the Twin Towers
from the roof of my building –
but not wanting to be a ghoul to other's misery
I went shopping,
keeping the morning angled at vague degrees.
On my way back I shared the elevator.
'Wasn't I gonna go up to see the accident? From 20 stories
it would be plain.'

Damn! I'd left my tobacco, so returned to the Deli
where there was talk of how collisions with buildings
roam our municipal psyche. Cited, was a small plane
in the late 30's colliding with the Empire State.
So back in my building after dropping the shopping
in my second floor studio, I went to the elevator
to confront King Kong apparent, and chogged skyward
(it's a city building with chogging city elevators)
to view a claustrophobic scene.

At two miles distance smoke billowed from serrated lips –
an actress smoking a cigarette for all seats,
expensive, non-expensive, in between.
The accident had happened
before the majority had arrived for work,
and lights ascending and descending
meant the elevators were in action.
So the situation seemed not entirely disastrous.
(Thus we interpreted information, surely not received.)

As we thought and sorted, a plane approached,
large as a hollyhock too much ablooming,
low over the river in the corners of our eyes.
Surely this plane would swoop
and in a manner non-adjacent to any previous maneuver,

let fall an all protecting shroud!
Yes, a powerful country keeps silent the meander of its caring!
This *must* be the explanation for the plane low flying,
on the lookout for some disease.

Instead – we felt the acceleration
(as much as we didn't want to)
of some intestine marvel howling
within the body of the plane.
The hope had been of an angel,
showing off an angel's strength.
Instead this plane, a trident belonging to a devil,
pulled the heart from witnesses,
rendering our testimony moot.
The explosion, birth of a world of entrails,
left the towers prey to a ravenous rationale with brains.

Other things happened. On the eighteenth floor,
in his own apartment – a man's corpse was discovered.
And as the first tower was falling
the social worker who'd unlocked his door
came to the roof for air.
Later, after the second tower had gone down
thousands walked up 1st avenue, unbandaged,
with disbelieving ways of smiling,
attempting to transcribe such damage.

A guy who, the previous evening, for the fourth time,
had abused and insulted me,
was waiting in the park to speak to me.
"Come around to sit. I won't hurt you.
Look what they've done to the two towers!"
he shouted through the railings
as I stood outside on a traffic island –
and the entrance to the park was a thousand miles
in the near distance,
communion between us so significant,
we'd never escape
the confines of our stares.

Mille-Feuille

The day after
Obama told us Osama
had been executed,
therefore wouldn't be appearing
impromptu in another video or film —
I attended a birthday party
                                       for a two year old.

This two year old
be-ringleted, be-ribboned,
gorgeous, blond,
is the adopted child
of two Queer Friends
(an affair of long standing)
one Jewish, one German
(her biological mother is New England Swedish,
biological father, Californian)
adopted before the exit from her Mother's tummy
                                       at minus 7 days old.

As she sits by the side of her German Dad
at her two year bash
the World claps —
her German Dad is *Poppa*,
her Jewish Dad, *Dada*,
and to continue this thematic internationalism
she's going to share a Mille-Feuille with her *Poppa*
who, speaking to her in German,
cuts a large half for her
                                       and a small piece
                                       for himself.

The surface of a Mille Feuille
known also as a Napoleon
(which has nothing to do with Napoleon
and for no anti-Napoleonic reason
is designated a Mille Feuille)
the surface of this pastry
                                       is nothing but icing.

Underneath the icing—3 layers of puff pastry
(puff pastry is flaky)
with layers of cream between.
BUT THIS UNDENIABLE ICING! Vanilla!
                                          Combed
                                          with chocolate!

The be-ribboned, be-ringleted,
commanded by appetite,
inadvertently destroying the underneath of the pastry,
tears the icing off and up, to her mouth,
which is waiting, and scoff gobbles.
                                          Only briefly
                                          her gobble is her grin.

For in the wobble of her gobble
she's confronted with the mess underneath the icing.
In the mess's middle
is Osama Bin Laden, laden with cream.
On the same confectionary latitude she comes across Hitler
yelling through flakes of puff pastry,
"Your fadders arrr not vearing dere stars!"
                                                "Eeets a sozial shame!"

The be-ribboned, be-ringleted
screams a red torture
and has to be cradled by *Dadda*, then *Poppa*,
by guests from numerous continents,
Queer and Straight.
Nothing can console her—for she's discovered
the mess under the icing.
Such enticement amounts
                                          to the devious
                                          perfections
                                          of the promised plate.

Extra Work

After a year of being ill — Cancer, HIV, Aching Brain —
      an assistant to an assistant to a casting director phones
offering me work as an extra on a film.
      Would I like to be a patient in a mental institution?
The location is a disused hospital,
      a quarantined area for some kind of spent plague.

The call is 1pm. A van is to meet us in Union Square.
      When the van arrives, 90 minutes late,
a production assistant swings his pigtail
      as if he's right on the knuckle of God's arranged time.
He doesn't know where we're going.
      "North," is all the driver's told him.
The length of our employment is uncertain.
      As yet, the film to be worked on has no name.
Such discombobulation is to be expected.
      Why should we have the grounding of a destination
when, as extras, all that's required
      is to creep beneath the eardrums of the dialogue,
vanish beneath the circumference of the lens
      and, if our imagination *is* recognized,
use less than one percent of its extent.

Not aware of where we are going, we are happy to be knowing
      we are crossing the George Washington Bridge.
From a highway we turn into a byway where stucco mansions
      are anxious to be palaces.
"Look!" screeches one of the extras (there are four of us)
      "That's the house where Betty Grable
had problems with her ankles because of drink!"
      "There's where Rock Hudson created ripples on the
nipples of pre-pubescent swimming pools, and boys did grin!"
      Road dives, banks rise,
we're on a level with the daisies in the parks of these estates.
      Peering through the daisies
we seek delusions of current reputations —
      myths of stars in the dimming, stars long dimmed —

myths which, though geometrical,
           are not overburdened with precision.

At the location, the former hospital, nothing is in order.
           Doorways are too broad to be entrances,
light gallops away from windows that let nothing in.
           An assistant director gives me the once-over,
decides I'm right to play a Remorseful Crazy
           in an inner courtyard.
He tells me I am resourceful to have brought along my cane.

Myself and another extra are ushered to the courtyard,
           gigantic, maintained,
where another assistant director passionately confides,
           "You're disturbed, as well as mental!" —
instructing the other extra,
           "You're his attendant." —
then disappearing as if he's provided dynamite for an explosion
           at the fiery center of which, we are the emotional vent.
The guy playing my attendant,
           an Italian American from Queens,
scratches his testicles (if he sees me watching,
           he'll scratch again)
and tells me the story of how he was told
           "If you speak Arabic, the part is yours." He'd replied,
"If you give me the part, I'll speak Arabic.
           Words are only names."

Knots of the crew jostle around the camera
           in the courtyard corner.
They want an 'establishing' shot, an 'uncomplicated' shot.
           They keep it vague.
Our job is to walk away from the camera. Up an avenue.
           Oaks on a lawn. Oaks atop a bank. We walk between.
To achieve a precise anonymity,
           the scene must be repeated ad infinitum.
We walk away from the camera,
           up an avenue,
away from the camera,

up an avenue.
        "DON'T WALK IN THE CENTRE!"
"STEER TO THE EDGE!"
        "YOU ARE NOT THE FUCKIN' STARS!"
"DON'T HOG THE SCENE!"
        The guy from Queens looks me up and down.
"You're English," he says. "Anybody ever tell you
        you're the image of Michael Caine?"
Veer from the camera.
        Up an avenue.
I let him know he's the spit of Brando,
        with Brando's pain.

Water Boarding

"Is Water Boarding torture?"
They'll tie you down as if playing a prank,
cover nostrils eyes mouth with a raggedy mask,
pour water down the throat till
believing in a minute you will be dead from drowning,
you'll convert from Straight to Queer, Buddhist to Muslim,
embrace what's postulated.
Oh, you'll agree.

I don't discuss this with a woman who might be a customer
outside the antique stall on Third and Houston,
its goods displayed on the sidewalk —
tiffany with toffee taste,
pink lover's seat,
lobster fresh from Maine.
Other goods
seen through cracks in the accompanying building
are uncertain articles from stylish domains.
She's leering at an object leaning against chicken wire.
Behind this object, behind the wire,
a truly absconded toilet seat, and a cracked mirror —
forever separated by a patch of weeds.

And the object itself?
A 3D nativity.
Neither sculpture, nor picture, nor in between,
it has the three Kings, Jesus, Mary, Joseph
in leaden plastic framed —
their heads painted a luscious bilberry, a mingled strawberry,
with cream bodies in cream robes, the cradle cream.
She asks, "Is this thrown out? I'll snap this up in a minute.
If it's free."

"Is an administered injection crueler, more inhuman
than the chair?"
Observers have noted agony,

with a realization that the color of the breath
you are incapable of breathing
is the color of the end. This
the woman (who is not really a customer) and myself
don't speak of.
We have that about us which we *can* discuss—
Avatar, Lady Gaga, Fighting Monster Sponges—
but nothing which might suggest, "Is injection superior
to electricity?"

Amish Country

1.
Every year our building (a senior citizen's building)
arranges a bus trip to Amish country in Pennsylvania—
Lancaster County.
The best time to go is late summer,
but this year the trip was arranged for the 31st of October,
October's last day.
Tickets were 25 dollars. Parker and myself decide to go
even though we can't afford it.
We're always strapped for cash.

The day starts at 8:30 with coffee and doughnuts in the lobby.
Then what should be a 3hr journey turns into 5
cuz there is a freak snow storm.
The bus has no heating and there's no paper in the lavatory,
and then the lock on the lavatory self-locks—
the whole bus has to hold their pee.
The driver tires of this condition and pulls over.
There, where late summer's leaves, hedges, and fields
are laden with snow,
the land wants to know, "Who's to blame?"

At the restaurant we arrive late, therefore
our reserved tables have been taken.
The meal is the high point of the trip.
Parker has been ill, with no appetite.
It is a pleasure to see him eat.
The food is tasty, but there is no help
with its journey to the belly.
In spite of checkered tablecloths,
the restaurant is about as intimate as an airplane hanger
and, as course follows course, the hanger grows larger
and larger.
We expect to be X-rayed, searched, hoarded on to planes.

After the meal we slush over
to the indoor Amish food market.
The Amish behind their stalls are withdrawn and rustic.
Amish men wear suspenders, which pull up their trousers

to show off their figures.
Parker loves the women in loose dresses
which don't disguise their big-boned frames.
Titillation is not prevalent, but the Amish do have
a grave exoticism going on beneath unadorned fashions,
which they insist are "plain".
I'd like to add—while the Amish make a habit of *withholding*,
the We that travel in the bus have a habit of *flaunting*,
of posing—presenting our separation
on private pedestals.
Do we enjoy this as persistently
as the Amish enjoy being grave?

2.
Years ago I worked in a summer theatre in this vicinity.
One night everybody in the show was invited for drinks
by a couple with a giant TV.
They played a DVD of the film 'Witness'
in which detective Harrison Ford has an Amish girlfriend.
Guests were allowed to do as they wanted.
A stage manager re-played the scene in Philadelphia Station
over and over again.
One of the actors present shouted, "Give me a break!
No! Not again."

3.
In the early years of this century there was a tragedy.
A gunman entered a one room Amish school
and after executing 5 girls and wounding 5 others,
killed himself with a shot to the brain.
These one-roomed schools are easy to get into.
He murdered children, wounded children, killed himself
quicker than he could say what it was he didn't believe.

The Amish took down the school
and built another, similar,
yet different from the one where the shooting had occurred.
In their horse-drawn buggies they occupy a zone
where Rage is not written into Bible, Law, or Constitution.
So some Amish attended the murderer's funeral.
Revenge is a serpent that lives in untilled ground.

There's a period of two years in the life of Amish adolescents
when, if they want, they may dress
in the vestments of the life outside.
There are those who experiment with Drugs
and Sex and Rock and Roll,
but the majority return, stable or unstable,
to the Amish fold.

4.
On the way home, our driver gets lost
and drives the wrong way up a highway.
Luckily we are being forced backward by a fresh blizzard
and in this state of non-collision our return proceeds.
Suddenly Philadelphia appears.
"Where have you come from?" snarls Philadelphia.
"You shouldn't be near me!"
—as our bus careens (perhaps) in the right direction.
Who is to say?

August Visitor To The Pacific Northwest

visitors

to the pacific northwest coast
don't see the sea

cliffs, trees in a general wind
hide it with their gentle sway

until at the end of an unimportant wood
a beach is exposed at a level with the road

*

laden

came I
with medications 'gainst HIV

"Decades of giant fucks
have made me statuesque enough
to be a visitor to the Pacific coast,"

I explain to a giant fog of water
the water breathes

*

blue pill

colored purple death pills
open your heart pills
on the table
before the cliff top drop

on my knees before that table

with my eyes close to the table's edge
the pills are giant lozenge flowers

idly floating on an ocean
doing its level best unflappable
to appear appeased

More Visitors To The Pacific Northwest

A family occupies a chalet
near other chalets
near a brook
that runs to the Pacific across some sand.
In the swimming pool of this facility
the Father of the family
teaches his Three Daughters
what it is to swim in water
as opposed to floating on land.
From the pool's edge, the Gorgeous Father
like a prophet, lifts, throws his Daughters
squarely smashing.
Someone non-religious mentioned —
"Baptism is synonymous with damage
in swimming pool, ocean, lake or font."

        Across the highway
        outside a forest
        a Veteran Youngster
        and a Budding Patriarch
        loiter at a sign —
        "Woodland Path".
        Discovering there is no trail,
        they wander among fallen trunks.
        Sounds of water
        magnify sounds of traffic.
        Is looking deep into a situation
        tantamount to being lost?

On the cliff a modern edifice peers down
while chalets in the forest lap eyelashes with flirtatious glance.
A Japanese Lover sleeps on the terrace
viewed by the Ocean.
Inside a Splendid Divorcee naps on her sofa.
It's her house.
The Lover is delighted with sleep's adulation
which fades him into a grey steel fluctuation

of cloudy water, watery cloud.
The house is lofty
on account of non-communion
(silent phones sit easy)
—though always they press on each other's senses
with his bare torso, her red pants.

> In a traditional house with mirrors
> a Host prepares
> a recreant avocado dip.
> In the evening,
> glass reflecting the Pacific
> will reflect
> *Youth with Patriarch,*
> *Lover with Divorcee,*
> *Family that swims.*
> In this cold August
> the Host is dressed for early winter.
> In his antique glass collection
> there is, for every guest,
> a glass of different century and shape.
> If this Host is manifold of anything
> he's manifold of means.

On the beach after dinner
Host,
Family that swims,
Youth with Patriarch,
Lover with Divorcee,
all stand in awe of the body of a Fish that in death
retains its glamour—an Enormous Ray.
This Fish's Wife had no understanding
that her husband's wish while dying
was to be transported outside the Ocean.
"Is this rational?
From the water famous for your dance,
you want your darling body to recline on earth
where suffocation lies?"

Visitors to the Pacific,
south of Canada,
north of Patagonia,
find this Fish,
in its dead state,
ascetic —
though not due to the miracle
of loaves and fishes,
but because a Fish on the beach
in a dead state
provides a limit
finite as beauty,
available as sand.

4
CHANGING

Let me go over your good gifts
That crown you queen;
A queen whose kingdom ebbs and shifts
Each week, Faustine.

— Swinburne

Changing

Last January I met a woman who enjoyed my being older
and declared she could get into the inner life of me
if, instead of jockies, I wore her panties in the summer
and in winter put on her long drawers—
so I wore her long drawers on her long bed in the night
and twisting with anxiety I woke up alright.

In Spring she instructed me to prance around the apartment
in her slip and brassiere
and if I didn't want her to hurt me
I'd better keep them on under my clothes.
Out of sheer initiative I stole her suspender belt and garters
from a drawer she rarely went into.

These she had discarded—
but I believe stockings have a worldlier-wise lustre
than panty hose.
Of course we couldn't remain in this condition.
We aren't a couple who stays indoors.

In early Summer, to show me how to walk,
she took me to her kitchen
where she stood me on the table to issue me commands.
I achieved a loose woman's squiggle
held together by a thread connecting my knees to my nipples
and my nipples to my jaw.
This was just what she wanted and she was ever so pleased!
By the Autumn could I be prepared to meet
the Men of her Company
and at the end of October make myself beautiful
and drive over for Halloween?

On the way I had a to-do with a cop—
"After tailing you I have to say that
you are out of the ordinary.
That's why you got stopped."
"Officer, are you referring to these denim mules
with the high platforms
which cause insensitivity between me

and the accelerator pedal
and thus dangerously increase my speed?"

At my girlfriend's party her boss smooths the flesh of my back
under my straps.
My girl promises me perfumes, lotions,
and to introduce me internationally
—*if* I do what her boss demands.
In a quiet corner the realization that my genitalia
are just co-incidental
is a thunder that claps.

I have to take comfort where I can obtain it—
so with pragmatic romanticism, I keel over
and end up slap in the boss's lap.
We experience ourselves as an entity.
When he winks, we kiss. When he jokes, we laugh.

As he lives by the dictates of corporate intelligence,
he touches me in the same places on a two-times-weekly basis.
As he lives within the confines of a limited text,
"You're my number one slut," he tells me
on Wednesdays and Fridays.
And if happiness is the well-being of others,
I'm happy because my girlfriend has been promoted
and we're a success.

It's no different from any erotic union.
When we set out exploring, it's always a gambol.
Are we or are we not going to be freshly astounded
by what it is we lack or what it is we possess?

Helen's Gone

Helen of Troy and husband Menelaus have a son, Nicostratus
—Nico for short. By those in the know, this is known.
Menelaus is a specimen
with pectorals and biceps, buttocks and testicles
fresh from the gardens surrounding Olympus,

                        almost a God.

Nicostratus is the pre-pubescent spit of his father
with muscles to be decided, yet to grow.
Nico says again and again, "Dad, I love your pecs
as much as your biceps.
I want those pecs to be my very own."
Helen senses the attraction between Menelaus and Nico

                        as she sits
                        with these Narcissists
                        in a royal room.

Father and Son have the same blond hair
with sharp parting—this parting reminiscent
of the cut dividing the two cheeks of their asses
which is a preoccupation of Greek culture
as well as Greek government—

                        ascertaining
                        the edges of contours
                        without clothes.

When Helen runs off with Paris
she reasons, "Oh, let them get on with it.
Stroke the reflections. Kiss the mirrors.
I'm well out of *this* nuclear family." And the sails flail
as she boards the Trojan ship

                        because the wind
                        is going to be
                        very bold.

After she escapes, the breeze drops, and in the airless heat
Menelaus and Nico are left in the Palace
super-aware of the cocktail cabinet, the couch, the stairs
where Helen would descend to show off her gowns.
With the servants gone just after supper
they are suddenly aware that they have never been so

>   completely,
>   one to the other,
>   unmercifully alone.

After a few nights what has to happen, happens —
not in the stables, but in the main living quarters.
Menelaus strips starkers and leans back on the couch
to display his state of excitement. And Nico strips
to get on the couch along with his father, administering to Dad
a gigantic pleasure with the touch of a feather —
both experiencing

>   an ecstatic anxiety
>   ancient,
>   foretold.

Dad is in quite a state of frustration,
what with Mam running off with Paris.
The fact of the matter is — Dad's dick is a scythe to be honed.
When Menelaus pulls him to a bending position,
standing behind in order to penetrate,
Nicostratus looks back over his shoulder, implying —
"This,

>   this
>   is how it is.
>   This
>   couldn't be better.
>   In the middle
>   of turbulence,
>   this
>   is your home."

Helen Has Returned

As much as Father and Son enjoy messing about,
Menelaus has to break the sweet moment up.
He gives his son a smacker direct on the gob,

                puts on his battle dress,
                and sets out.

Menelaus is the King of Sparta, more a kingdom than a state,
and plenty are the heroes from other principalities

                who aid and abet,
                abet and sweat,

admiring each other's buttocks, or who has the best package,
for this is the era of primitive ancients, related to myth
by more than the skin of their teeth—

                designated sons
                of Gods and Godesses
                and horses and swans.

After ten glorious or inglorious years
(depending in whose day is written the story)
comes the greatest ruse in the History of Efficacy—
30 elite soldiers, tangled in eroticism's mystery,
are pulled deep into Troy

                in the belly
                of a horse.

Menelaus, who has chosen himself as one of the 30,
springs out and opens Troy's gate
to let in the rest of the Greeks—

                lithe in the night
                stretching in whatsoever direction
                to accommodate war.

He himself had been nestling where,
in a flesh and blood horse,
in the world of the concrete, just over the bollocks,

>   the kidneys
>   and the bladder
>   claim their position.

Through the great slaughterhouse landscape
Menelaus bounds to the Palace. With Paris dead,
Helen has taken up with Deiphobus,
Paris's younger brother —
therefore Menelaus knows the future (Virgil, Euripides, etc)
will have nothing to say for her.

>   He has license to kill.
>   Direct on the spot.
>   Then. There.

In her throne room, Hecuba,
the widowed grandmother Queen,
understands that the time has come
to massacre women and children —
all that's left, with the Trojan heroes dead.
She tells Menelaus
it's an awesome idea to begin with Helen
who stands alone in the disconsolate Palace

>   watching the fracas
>   from the terrace
>   of a state room upstairs.

At the balustrade Helen looks back at him over her shoulder.
He has his sword in his hand.
"You've come to kill me. I know I deserve it."
Helen is as innocent as her son Nicostratus

>   as he prepares
>   for penetrative sex.

She lets her gown open, she lets it fall
from her shoulders to carefully drape her undress.
From within its folds she brings out cigarette case and lighter.
"Do you want one? They're Turkish. I have them imported."

>   Significantly,
>   she lights her cigarette.

Years ago Menelaus gave up tobacco, but still he *is* tempted.
"How's Nico. By now he must be quite big."
How he enjoys the rise of her breasts' turreted tumults

                            as instead of inhaling
                            she allows the smoke to float in.

Under his gaze Helen grows older. His sword enlarges.
(His sword in intention is the strength of his penis.
Not used properly there'll be much to forgive.)
Are the signs of age—wrinkles?—the absence of twinkle?
He looks away to the battle over the balustrade.
When he looks back at her
he doesn't remember what he doesn't remember.
He knows only, by hell or high water, by all juxtapositioning,
he's taking her back home by galleon.

                            Or maybe by plane.

End Of The Affair

Let me tell you.
Do I want to tell you?
I'm going to tell you.

If there has to be a subject, it is passion—I've had my share.
One of these affairs whirled me in its vortex.
When in my 40's I fell for an Indian guy of
(I can hardly write it.) (Write it!) — 19.

Up to then I'd had relationships
at easy intervals
with my same color, age, level of libido—same.
And then comes Gappu, with a sensuality
that drowns the liquor,
smothers music, has me going back to clubs,
is the strong light of a 36 hour dawning—
which is to say hedonistic,
leaving no opportunity to examine political systems
or new diseases,
one of which I was to acquire —
Acquired Immune Deficiency Syndrome, AIDS.

My love reigns in terms of its beginnings —
Romeo & Juliet, David & Jonathan, getting their first eye full.
But I'd started late
and in bed our Hindu aerobics begin to grate,
expressing an excess of defeat.
"Holy Mary! Mother of Sex!"
I pray to be branded with non-desire,
a quick release.

It happens—
in a sophisticated bar where my Indian loved to drink.
HERE—HE SETS FIRE TO A MUTUAL GIRLFRIEND'S HAIR!
A fierce attachment had formed between him and this girl,
and sitting on adjacent stools her fringe goes up in flames
when she leans into him
as he leans into her
to light her cigarette.

The bar man rushes with soda siphon,
dousing the flames flaming from her cranium,
spraying the apparent unconscious in her face.
In drunkenness, the two of them collapse in laughter
as streams of soda water, mixed with cinders,
course down her forehead, neck and cheeks.

This soda is water from the River Lethe,
the River of Forgetfulness.
Flowing to the floor it becomes real deep,
enabling me to swim out the door, up through Manhattan.
With no sign of safety, such as a dingy,
I refuse to consider either of *them*—
though from time to time we meet.

From then on I got older,
more focused on innocence as a career.

Though my spontaneous head
bursting so often into fire
tops off my body—which like a hobnailed chrysalis
may still dream the licentious dream.

Thin Skinned

And on the seventh day after his sixth chemo Parker is so weak he has no choice in the matter — all he can do is rest. Chemotherapy is accumulative. So, of course, is space. Is the journey toward annihilation a journey to our zenith?

Back at his third chemo Parker began to live

                              in this place where nobody prays.

Today he has to go to the Cancer Centre for the result of the X-ray to discover if the lumps have formed into clumps or have been forced to disappear. I insist on going with him. He mumbles, — the doctors will think I'm his white boy friend, that he's a Black Queer Bi-sexual, an Ethnic who pays visits to White Homoland. — Well! The road of truth doesn't have to connect with facts. Facts are lanes which run in all directions.

Parker doesn't enter into this conversation.

                                        He has no breath.

Suffering is a gerund, a transference of the active (*he suffers*) into its substantial. *Pain* can be transferred from the substantial into its descriptive, e.g. *'I've got a pain'* into *'It's painful'* — also into the active *'It pains me'*. Between *Pain* and *Suffering*, I choose *Suffering*. — No. Let me change to *Pain*.

— No, I've changed again.

                    Between pain and suffering, I choose change.

Before he knows it, we are getting out of the cab (he's too weak for public transport) outside the Cancer Centre in Union Square. In Union Square there are too many people for this overcrowded century.

Across in the park, astounded autumn trees

                                      have too many leaves.

In the reception area there is a frail female patient and a fat male patient. Both of them possess an indestructibility that is only temporary, but which on this Friday morning

at 10:49 at the end of October

is on display.

Work Ethic

1.
An American writer I know makes a living with her voice
(commercials, voice-overs, dubbing).
It's a difficult area to get into,
crowded with performers who've been doing it
since they can't remember when
and who'd die rather than move over
to make a little more room.

She considers herself lucky
to have found an enjoyable occupation,
even though the field is so competitive
she believes every job will be her final shot.
"I'll never get another job," she bemoans,
but soon enough she finds something.
Suddenly there will be her voice on the subway —
"If you notice an unattended package, please report it."
 "Please mind the gap."

Needn't be in America. The Wide World Over
needs announcements in English.
Native English speakers traveling in distant countries
are as frightened by the foreign language
as they are by the foreign shore.

2.
A Scottish Buddy (his name is Buddy) is in his 80's.
He's a talented interior decorator who would be famous
except all he takes seriously is Sexy Love.

It's an area crowded with youngsters
holding onto their prerogatives.
Confounded, Buddy doesn't know what to do with
his in-your-face nipples,
his sensual acumen, his mesmeric touch.

When his last affair was over, he believed
he was on the rubbish heap, up in the attic,

a corpse in a tomb in the chapel of a forgotten cathedral
in an unpopular town.

Then, from out of nowhere,
he's contacted by this architectural surveyor from East Anglia
who wants the interior of his country house
to reflect the wild exterior.
Impressed with Buddy's talent,
he takes him to Ascot, to the Royal Enclosure,
then to the South of France
to taste the vintage of a small region —
and there Buddy meets the man of his life,
a wine grower with a really promising wine.

3.
My ex-boyfriend Danny
introduced me to a dominatrix in a venue up on 58th Street.
The dominatrix could only join us briefly
for she was due to descend
to the S&M facilities in the basement.
The jazzy exterior implied a jazz club —
yet upstairs it's a bar, while downstairs
the S's & the M's get their fix.

By day, she's head of admissions
in the Emergency Room of a well known hospital.
That's where Danny met her —
he was Admissions Clerk in the Eye Clinic
before it closed down.
Unemployed now,
Danny has taken on 'Immobility' —
he's become 'Sculptural' —
he's the 'Mermaid' on the wharf at Copenhagen's port.

And like the 'Mermaid', he's multi-dimensional,
which is more dimension than he wants.
Too bulky for the dock,
he's going to tip and cleave into the water
unless the dominatrix finds him a position.
She's on close terms with the club owner.
They're going to have a talk.
Dominating in the basement,

Danny will be able to concentrate on interiors
without perimeters—
not so different from Mermaids
looming in and out of focus
in the great North Sea,
spiraling to scenes untold.

Polish And Moroccan Constructions

1.

The first time I saw photos on a telephone was a year ago—when I met this skinny Polish Construction Worker. *'Call me Peter. Americans can't pronounce my name.'* He was so hungry I treated him to chicken over spicy rice from the neighborhood food cart. Normally he loitered over near the Chinese Church—waiting with Mexicans and Russians for a Chinese construction foreman who chose workers each day and took them to a non-union construction site in his shiny van. The morning I met him Peter was wandering and not working because the old Chinese guy hadn't turned up. Instead he'd sent his son. This son had chosen only Mexicans. According to Peter, *'Mexicans are good workers but tire easily. They don't last long.'*

Then out of his back pocket he pulled his phone and clicked on a photo of a hunk in a swimsuit—himself when muscular and young—standing beside a stretch of water frosty in texture. Is that Poland? *'It's the Ukraine. Look at the size of my arms and body. I swam across that water.'*

From somewhere—in the photo?—in the park?—there is applause and laughter. *'I swam it easily. I could do it today. I'm strong.'*

2.

The photo had battled with life's texture. It wanted to be a painting, rendering oblivion into permanence, the frail into the everlasting strong.

Another friend who carried such a painting in his back pocket was Yassar, a Moroccan intellectual. Both of us were living in Paris. We'd said *'hello'* to each other in the Pompidou Museum at an exhibition flaunting the relationship between Picasso and Cezanne. Like Pete, Yassar was penniless. Could he afford to eat? What was going to happen when he didn't have money for his room? He was ambidextrous sexually, so men *and* women used him. He managed to maintain his image as we wanted it. We all loved his beauty. We feasted on him, being no longer young or beautiful ourselves.

He had studied philosophy. One of his professors had been Michel Foucault. Michel Foucault had been a friend to everybody. If he'd still been alive, Yasser could no doubt have introduced me. This produced in me an attack of inadequacy. How lacking did I appear if Michel Foucault was Yasser's measure of a man?

3.

I went into the restaurant where Yasser was sometimes needed as a waiter, but that evening was working behind the bar. Yassar never expressed allegiance to the strict laws of Islam, in fact, he was shocked at nothing. If taken out to dinner, he would often choose pork. Sex and alcohol? *Pas de probleme!* As I was drinking my wine, I saw his phone lying on the counter. I picked it up and saw an image of Yassar in a farmyard garden, with the Atlas Mountains leaning beyond him, and a prayer mat on the ground.

In his phone, he was carrying around the mountains, the animals (there were goats), prayer (which is the same as hope — if it turns you on); and when he wanted it, this modernist in patched jeans and leather jacket switched on a reminder of himself wearing a *jellaba*. The photo was grainy, black and white — but within the image, details relieved of language told the unmentioned truths of his unmentioned town.

Rehab In Westchester

After a year of co-habitation,
Parker went back to drugs.
Rehab was mandatory.
He was sent to a town in Westchester,
the richest county in the State.

I'm asking myself—
"Can I be anyone's savior?"—
when I receive an envelope, with brochure.
DURING VISITS FRIENDS LOVERS HUSBANDS WIVES
SHOULD NOT ATTEMPT TO SOLVE
THE PATIENT'S PROBLEMS
SHOULD NOT MORALIZE.

On the train to Westchester
the alcoholic city presses 'gainst the window,
bridges do everything for themselves,
no switching of agreements twixt lower and higher rentals.
Bridges and rentals don't dish out blame.

Prevailing situation
is promising in the station,
railway leading
towards goals, aims.

Outside the station
I ask directions from a Gentleman parked next to a Laundromat.
Busy loading laundry into an imponderable limousine,
he treats me as a mass that lacks all fact.
His drug is perspicacity. I'm something to be nailed.

I explain,
"I'm looking for Saint Vincent's Rehabilitation Centre."
"Do you intend to walk?"
"Yes. This is Sunday. There is no bus on Sunday."
He's just noticed I have a cane.
"...straight across the bridge..."
Confusion is coagulating beneath his answer,

his accent (penetrable, predictable) providing protection
against the friendly gesture —
which would be to offer me a lift.

"The clinic is a quick fifteen minutes."
Yeah, by raft in an Egyptian frieze.

Several miles and an hour later
(it was a day with an afternoon that reached 95 degrees)
I'm passing mansion after mansion —
where extravagant gables watch sculptured gardens
with plants of extraordinary geometry.
Who cares for these plants?
Humans encapsulated in their motors
are the only humans to be seen.

I have to find someone
with some notion
that the clinic exists.

Don't think about stopping a car.
Stopping a car is akin to opening a grave.
I walk into a courtyard driveway,
paved in astonishing marble,
towards a low slung mansion —
and knock a knocker on a door the size of gates.

Behind, to the side, there is the movement of a curtain.
That curtain moved! Behind glazed glass
a blazed lover shifted anonymously
to create a complicated drink.

I try next door.

There, a Swiss Gothic castle
proffers plants from the shadows of Ghana
to the highest reaches of Peru
as cars pass and no birds fly
and roses expose some corrosive lie.
A thirty-year-old keeper of the inn comes towards me
from beyond the boundaries of her property,
the nether region of some woods.

Sorry to confuse her,
I promise not to solve her problems for her,
assuring her that at the end of our relationship
we will retain our independence.
"Can you inform me...? Am I going in the direction of...?"

She murmurs.
"The clinic's three minutes up the road."

It's not tit for tat.
I have done nothing for her.
When I came knocking she was hoping
for a fighting power to lessen the Mighty Load.

In de-tox reception
a receptionist guard brandishes Information:
"Before the visit you will be shown a video on the effect of the drug on the addict, the effect of the addict on the addict, to explain the drug's effect on the drug's effect on the affected scene."

In the logbook,
a third column demands
that the names of Patient and Visitor
be tripled
with a named Relationship.

                          Atop the page:

PATIENT	***VISITOR***	***RELATIONSHIP***
typed	overbold	a mite too plain.

Saint Vincent

St. Vincent's Hospital (which saved my life)
has been closed down because of Bankruptcy.

The Main Building on 12th street is post-operative pale.
Only days ago there was so much energy,
façade flushed rouge.
Now, without guards on duty,
I stalk into the interior—empty of furniture.
Will I clog the toilets which are arteries?
Will I kick walls so blood will be drawn?

On the third floor is a door of tattered mahogany.
Here the smell of dust and thorns.

This is one of the hospital's theatrical lavatories.
I force the door. When I open a window,
I hear a trickle of asphyxiation,
a spit of gore.
Behind me on the throne of the privy is St. Vincent,
who gave his name to this hospital,
who founded the 'Sisters of Charity' to serve the sick poor.
Except for a cornette (Sally Field's headdress)
he's bollock naked,
proud to be ancient,
confused and alone.

Since the seventeenth century
St. Vincent's been working here daily—
so he takes me on a tour.

In what was *urology* he shouts,
"Watch me thread this needle up my very large penis."
In *gynecology*,
"Appraise my mound of Venus."
In *podiatry*,
"Smile as you clean between my toes."
These activities, he explains, are typical of healers—
preening his healer's body consisting of sores.
St. Vincent then screams, "What is being done to me?"

I ask, "Do you have all your faculties?"
"That's a trick question. I need to adjust my colostomy bag."

I can't stay talking.
I have an appointment with my HIV doctor.

The HIV clinic is housed in a building across 7th Avenue,
the only clinic to remain.
Exam tables, scales, IV stands, walkers, crutches, water fountains
—all strewn on the sidewalk,
they enjoy a mingled communion
lacking inside the hospital,
when they were separated by people,
separated by disease.

The clinic is tucked away
in a ground floor corner
of this large eight story structure,

preparing to sail to the river.
Constructed as the headquarters of the Maritime Guild,
it's a ship disguised.
A main corridor leads to a deck
where sits another St. Vincent—
there are billions, one per building,
this one similar to the one previously spied.
"What is being done to me?" squeals St. Vincent
as the ship starts to quiver.
The Captain comes over.
"You've been experimenting sexually, century after century.
Your penance is the wrench of the tempest's roar."

Taste

A guy I had an affair with 50 years ago comes to stay with me for a couple of weeks in New York. Well into our sixties, we were vigorous homosexuals. Now, in our seventies, we're less vigorous (he's a year older than me) but we're still bold.

Because of his convictions he's been a great influence, a custodian of culture rather than a mentor, a discriminator of what is to be chucked from what has been accrued.

That first night I take him to the Opera. The work is way over-the-top, but I think he'll accept its hot surprises as he tends to equate over-statement with a rejection of the rote.

Instead, he sits torturing his chest into puckered breasts, as if what is on the stage is a wounded animal with whom he can't commiserate or connect.

What transpired? — He himself was hurt.

Afterwards, at dinner, he tells me he used to think there was something lacking in Opera as a convention. Now he feels *he's* lacking as a convention.

"I'm intellectually paltry," is his self-castigation. "I'm no more than a sexless apolitical endeavor, a fanciful concoction not well endowed."

The day after we go to the Met to visit the new galleries of Greek and Roman sculpture—and thanks to the Classical, the mood bazooms. In the 30,000 square foot space we gambol with lascivious sprites. In the Olympics we celebrate physical bodies and make our bodies proud. Our exterior grace manifests our interior wisdoms, and our interior wisdoms have buttocks to die for and nipples so ripe if you tweaked them, our chests would implode. Even when less than whole, armless, noseless, cockless, the bone of our eccentricity remains erect—and what is beautiful, endures.

Pagan Rights

I return to Wales to do a couple of poetry readings,
and I stay with my Catholic sister.
My being Queer
and Queer being the subject matter of my poems
upsets her.
I'm part of the Heathen take-over of the town.
5 houses up are Heathen drug dealers.
On their way to make purchases,
Pharisees pass in front of *her* window,
along *her* road.
Yet when police cars drive up and police enter *that* house
(the dealers have been reported)
nobody is arrested.
When heathens get off scot-free, my sister is distraught.

She instructs that on weekends
I must steer clear of the high street.
Saturday nights, teen crack addicts get high in the town centre
before they have sex in the park.
Sundays they have sex again.
Tiring of the solitary partners of the previous night,
they move on to the bus station to do it in gangs.

On *my* teenage Saturdays
we would walk around Woolworth's, go to the movies,
drink a couple of drinks, go to the dance in the town hall.
Sundays we'd go from church to church.
In the Welsh Chapel an abundant bosom
was the exalted feature
of the exhuberant female pedaling the organ.
Tight pants showed off the ample Christian packages
of Christian Choir boys
between the lines of psalms.

If I don't stay with my sister, I stay in Cardiff
with an artist who is becoming well known.
When he bothers to read my poems, he says they are retarded.
He wants graphic descriptions ala William Burroughs.
He wants the unseen real ala Wallace Stevens.

He refers to dozens of poets' poems that I don't know.

This earthy earth demanded I be educated Christian.
If the facilities had been available
I could have followed Buddhism,
read the Talmud,
belonged to Islam —
most anything would have been OK
as long as it was *not* Pagan!
Pagan is anarchist semen in the depths of the bollocks
preparing to shoot at the paper
whereon is the poem whose crackling testicles
issue an illiterate bellow.
My sister states that this is a criminal hand job.
My artist friend believes it's a shoot at the moon.

The Bottom Of Christopher Street

At the bottom, Christopher Street meets a highway.
On the other side is the Hudson.
The flow is undetectable. It ain't going nowhere.
Journey near complete, I cross over and walk out onto the pier.
In the seventies this pier was ready to fall into the water,
it was so decayed.
This was the area for Homo Roaming.
Nobody asked 'will you marry me?'
as the pier collapsed into the river,
as we let our bodies have their sway.
This new pier has rails, not walls,
and so is open to all elements.
It's a meeting place for Teeny-Pervs, for Hooli-girlie-gans
whose parents have chucked them to the wolves
that haunt the democratic streets.

A few miles down is Lucy Liberty, the famed cross-dresser
who stands where the river is neither bay nor river,
the bay not yet a bay.
Her real name's Larry.
This is revealed when she turns towards New Jersey. Nightly,
on the sly, with her back turned toward us,
she is on the look-out for foreigners.
Instead of acquiescence
she blares a question not based on the American
or any other kind of dream.

Lucy wants to know:
"WHAT'S THE NAME OF THIS WATER?"
"Strip of Water," comes an uneducated reply.
A more educated voice proffers,
"This is the estuary meeting the Atlantic."
Lucy Liberty instructs,
"WHEN I ASK A QUESTION, I PROVIDE THE ANSWER.
I'M THE ONLY ONE PRESENT
NOT INCLINED TO OVERPONDER."
She opens her lips and sexily hisses:
                    "SEA."

Photo by: Stas Pix

ABOUT THE AUTHOR

John Marcus Powell is a poet who is also an actor. Born in Wales, he has lived in London, Paris, Rome, Algeria, and for the past twenty-five years in New York City. His career as an actor spans British Rep, British soaps (as a doctor on ITV's *Emergency Ward 10*), American horror movies (*Metamorphosis: The Alien Factor*), London's West-End (*Zigger-Zagger* & Ian McKellan's understudy in *The Promise*), Off-Broadway (*The Comedians* & *Perfect Crime*), and Off-Off-Broadway (*Hedda Gabler* & *The Visit*). He was directed by Harold Pinter in Robert Shaw's *The Man In The Glass Booth* in London. Pinter encouraged his writing, and helped him get his short stories published in Joe McCrindle's *Transatlantic Review*. He is the author of the chapbook, *Loonie Lovers (Exot Books, 2012)*, and continues to perform his poetry extensively in New York City. As a poet he tap-dances to the rhythms of verse and prose, boogies through transgression, jives with socialism, square-dances with queerness, and flirts with any anarchic poet he's ever met—particularly Whitman, Shakespeare, Rimbaud, and Dickensen.

OTHER TITLES AVAILABLE FROM EXOT BOOKS

A Special Education, *Meredith Bergmann* ~ 2014
Questions, *Richard Loranger/Bill Mercer* ~ 2013
Turn, *Ann Drysdale* ~ 2013
Tomorrow & Tomorrow, *David Yezzi* ~ 2013
Facing The Remains, *Tom Merrill* ~ 2012
Blue Wins Forever, *Paco Brown* ~ 2012
They Can Keep The Cinderblock, *Mike Lane* ~ 2012
Colors, *Jay Chollick* ~ 2011
Loony Lovers, *John Marcus Powell* ~ 2011
Filled With Breath: 30 Sonnets by 30 Poets, *ed. Mary Meriam* ~ 2010
Let Me Be Like Glass, *Adriana Scopino* ~ 2010
What's That Supposed To Mean, *Wendy Videlock* ~ 2010
We Internet In Different Voices, *Mike Alexander* ~ 2009
11 Films, *Jane Ormerod* ~ 2008
Aquinas Flinched, *Rick Mullin* ~ 2008
Graceways, *Austin MacRae* ~ 2008
Prospero At Breakfast, *Alan Wickes* ~ 2008
Sometime Before The Bell, *Ray Pospisil* ~ 2006
The Countess Of Flatbroke, *Mary Meriam* ~ 2006
Blue Glass Cities, *Mark Allinson* ~ 2006
Prolegomena To An Essay On Satire, *R. Nemo Hill* ~2006
William Montgomery, *Quincy R. Lehr* ~ 2006

ORDER ONLINE AT ~ www.exottreasures.com/exotbooks

www.ingramcontent.com/pod-product-compliance
Ingram Content Group UK Ltd.
Pitfield, Milton Keynes, MK11 3LW, UK
UKHW041306180426
11947UKWH00009B/712